"High school can be a tough time in a person's life. It can be hard to fit in, find friends, and most importantly find yourself. For Willie Burton, after a life of growing up different from his friends, walking different, talking different, he didn't know what he was going to find at Fairfield High School. What he found was just what he needed. Besides finding a wrestling room where he felt at home, he also found a family in his teammates. Willie's story is one that we all can learn from. And there is a reason that Willie walks and talks differently than others—he is a wrestler. And he's earned the distinction."

—Dan Lindberg, Feature Producer – *E:60* | *ESPN*

"When I interviewed Willie on my show on Takedown Wrestling I pointed out to the listeners that he was born differently than some of us, with him having cerebral palsy, but he didn't let it stand in the way or hinder his love of competition. Disability is only in the eye of the beholder, and Willie proves it again and again. His life story is an inspiration not only to those with handicaps but to anyone who must overcome any challenges in their own life."

—Scott Casber, Sr. Vice President, *Takedown Media*

"Willie Burton was born a fighter. Entering the world two months prematurely and weighing two and a half pounds, the tiny child with cerebral palsy and a crack cocaine addiction was not exactly the perfect baby his adoptive parents, Brenda and Larry Burton, had in mind. Trusting in God's provident care, they took their child home, resolved to give him a better life than the odds suggested. Supported by Brenda's love and encouragement through years of hospitalizations and physical therapy, Willie tackled every challenge put before him. The teen faced the ultimate test, though, when his determination to earn a place on his high school's wrestling team put everything on the line. He relied on his faith in God to help him prove that life would not ever pin him to the mat!"

—Karen Kuhlman, Northern Kentucky columnist

Heart of a Lion–

Our Journey of Faith and Courage

Willie and Brenda Burton
with Barry Kienzle

Headline Books, Inc.
Terra Alta, WV

Heart of a Lion –
Our Journey of Faith and Courage

by Willie and Brenda Burton with Barry Kienzle

To order additional copies of this book or for book publishing information, or to contact the author:

Headline Books, Inc.
P. O. Box 52
Terra Alta, WV 26764
www.headlinebooks.com

Tel: 304-789-3001
Email: mybook@headlinebooks.com

Cover photo by Angie Matos Photography

ISBN: 9781946664778

Library of Congress Control Number: 2019946845

PRINTED IN THE UNITED STATES OF AMERICA

In honor of Clarence Adrian Puckett, 1925-2016

This book is dedicated to my Grandpa Puckett, a man who taught me about respect, strength, and honor. Without his influence and guidance, I wouldn't be the man I am today. He was the proud owner of Puckett's Auto Service for many years and served in the Army in World War II.

Although I never had the privilege of knowing him during his working years, I've heard many wonderful stories of what an honorable and great man he was throughout his entire life.

So Grandpa, while you are no longer with us, I want to thank you for being a role model and guiding light to me, and an example of how to be a true man. My greatest accomplishment in life will be if I can be like you.

I love you, Grandpa. This is for you.

Willie

Foreword
by Dan Gable

As I read Willie's amazing life story to date, I want to know what's next. So many obstacles were and are in front of this young man, yet his attitude and actions have driven him to success. Since Willie chose wrestling in his life, and wrestling *is* my life, I'm writing this foreword. Wrestling is one tough life lesson sport that gives its participants the knowledge  and the edge that make successful differences throughout their lifetimes.

The battle is more important than the results, at least for Willie in his career. The application of all the preparations has carried him to some high-level performances. This will still be needed as he continues to proceed in life.

His story is not over for he will continue to face extraordinary challenges. The only difference is time, for over time, the world evolves and more opportunities are developed and discovered.

What this book gives its readers is inspiration at its highest. Success and winning often give inspiration, yet here the struggles are doing that in Willie's life.

Willie's story is great but challenging. This book helps us all.

Content

Prologue

"For I know the plans I have for you," declares the Lord,
"plans to prosper and not to harm you, plans to give
you hope and a future."
—*Jeremiah 29:11*

I'm Willie Burton. When I was young, I wanted to run and jump and play like other kids, despite suffering from the debilitating aftereffects of cerebral palsy. Physical activities were a challenge for me, but that didn't prevent me from taking them on. I had an attitude that I wanted to be the best. I wasn't always sure at what, but I was always giving it my all at whatever I was doing.

It's hard to get ahead in today's world, especially if you have disabilities, but I'm not complaining, it just means I need to work harder to get what I want. At the same time, physical challenges allow some to accomplish great things while simply preventing others from leading what would be considered a normal life. It's still up to us.

It's important not to let your disability define you. Some people automatically form judgments about those suffering from disabilities, both physical and mental. It's easy to categorize us by what we can't do, which places a stigma on us. We're often not viewed as "normal," and many often pity the disabled.

But those of us with disabilities don't view ourselves as victims. We are given an opportunity to excel – to overcome! We look at what we must accomplish to achieve our goals, whether it is to walk, to dress, to feed ourselves, or to just survive in a world designed for those less physically challenged. A better measurement for someone with a disability is how they deal with or overcome adversity, which often is just coping with their limitations.

In the end, I found wrestling, or maybe it found me. It gave me a mountain to climb and a way to do it and would help turn me into the man I've become. But the true essence of my story isn't about wrestling at all; it just played out on that stage. It's about triumphing over adversity. Overcoming the challenges life throws at me is the essence of my life. How much can one person take before they crumble under the stress?

I owe a tremendous debt of gratitude to my adoptive parents, especially my mother, Brenda, who gave of herself to raise a special needs child and still cares for me today. My story is as much hers as it is mine. Without her love, devotion, and direction I may have fallen by the wayside in my dream of being as good as I can be.

Many have told me they admire my willpower to accomplish what I have. But it takes more willpower to do what she and my father have done than it does for me to crawl out onto a mat to wrestle. In my opinion, her burden is ten times harder than mine. My gratitude continues to all of the others who believed in and joined my struggle in so many different ways.

There aren't many times when someone with a physical disability doesn't feel they're not being judged by others, but when I was on the wrestling mat, I didn't feel I was being judged. Kyle Maynard, the well-known wrestler from Georgia who was born with congenital amputation where his arms ended at his elbows and his legs at his knees, said it best: "When you're on the mat it doesn't matter about your race, what you look like, or your abilities. During your match, you're just a wrestler, and that's all that matters." I lived by that philosophy.

Many believe God never sends us more than we can handle, but He does have a way of testing our limits. Sometimes it's hard to find our way, but if we have Faith and believe in Him, He'll lead us if we let Him.

Johnny Miller, the famous golfer, now announcer, once said, "It's not so much what you accomplish in life that really matters, but what you overcome that proves who you are, what you are, and whether you are a champion." We all face challenges in our lives. It's just a matter of how we work toward overcoming them that gives us the energy to push on.

This is mine and my mother's story—one of faith and courage. As you'll see, there's nothing "normal" about it. As I approach adulthood, I'll be faced with many new and different challenges. But I'll take them on and search for those who will help guide me and I know the Lord will continue to show me the way.

1

My Call To Wrestling

Whatever you do, work at it with all your heart,
as if working for the Lord.

—*Colossians 3:23*

Willie:

"Is this where the wrestlers meet?" I hesitantly asked another student approaching the gym after school on the first day of wrestling practice.

"Yes," he replied, sizing me up, no doubt wondering why a kid like me, in a wheelchair, would be asking such a question. As I rolled into the gym the atmosphere was eerily quiet – like everyone there knew what was coming next but me. I expected a rowdier bunch and their serious looks increased my anxiousness more than ever.

The head coach, Coach Toeupu Liu, approached the silent group and no one stirred. I could feel the uneasiness cover them like a fog. His eyes scanned the group, no doubt looking for the new faces as well as those returning from last year's team.

He began to speak in a serious tone about the rigors of wrestling and announced it is a very tough sport that's not meant for everyone. He went on to explain how we would be pushed to our limits both physically and mentally. The first week would be a test to see who could cut it which he punctuated by announcing that half of the group would most likely be gone by the end of the week.

I wondered whether his comment improved or hurt my chances of making the team. But suddenly, the reality of my new adventure hit me like a ton of bricks and I began to question my decision to sign up for the wrestling team at all. I squirmed nervously in my chair.

This wasn't what I had expected, but I didn't have anything to compare it to. I thought it would just be a bunch of jocks yukking it up and getting on with practice. I had never been on any organized team, so I didn't know what to expect from the coaches, either.

Yet here I was, a kid in a wheelchair with cerebral palsy who had little use of his legs, and the challenge of a very weak right arm, being told that half of us wouldn't make it past the first week. *What was I thinking when I signed up? Who would do such a thing? Had I bitten off more than I could chew?* Sometimes you just have to let life come to you. At the same time, I couldn't know then how wrestling would come to change my life forever.

***

I'm not the type of person who plans every detail of their life, but many have asked how I chose wrestling, such a physically demanding sport, at all. Few could have anticipated it and I would expect most would be curious about my decision. I've always thought it may have picked me, rather than my picking it or perhaps the guiding hand of the Lord decided it was the right thing at the right time for me. Who knows?

I'm sure the other kids there checking me out didn't know that sports already played a big role in my life, much bigger than I could have ever imagined. By *big*, I'm referring to the positive effect they had on my life through my interest and participation in them. Sports have given me a vehicle for physical activity while allowing me to compete with others at various levels. No doubt I wouldn't have had an interest in wrestling if I hadn't been interested in sporting competition in general.

I craved physical activity from an early age but not those types of sports where everyone got a trophy or a medal at the end of the season just for participating. That's often how sports for the disabled as well as other groups are structured. I liked competitive sports - I wanted to earn it.

My driving force was to compete where I had a chance to be considered the best. It didn't mean I would achieve it, but I wanted to be able to compete for it, to feel fulfilled by my attempts. I wanted challenges and obstacles to overcome in sports where I had to work hard every day to earn it. That's what got my juices flowing. If I excelled, great, and if I didn't, then I worked even harder to try to get better.

I've always been super competitive, it's my nature, maybe to a fault. If you challenged me on anything, I was going to try to beat you. It didn't matter what it was.

Sometimes there's a fine line between a virtue and a vice. I'm not always sure where the fire in my belly falls, but given what I've had to overcome in my life, I think my competitive spirit has been more of a virtue than a vice for me.

***

I didn't know much about wrestling beforehand when I was young. Sure, I watched WWE events on TV, but that's showmanship and theatrics and not wrestling in its purest form, the way it's performed in high schools and colleges, or in the Olympics.

Some middle schools have wrestling, but mine didn't, so it wasn't until I reached Fairdale High School near Louisville in my freshman year that I had any inkling of the dynamics of the real sport. I was attending freshman orientation when a pamphlet on display on the wrestling team's table caught my attention. It had *Bulldog Wrestling* written in bold letters, so curious, I picked up one.

I looked it over and immediately told Mom I wanted to wrestle, though I knew very little about the sport. I knew I just wanted to be a Bulldog wrestler. It sounded tough and exciting which appealed to me. She gave me the typical mother's answer of, "We'll see what we can do." I think she thought she stymied my interest, but she hadn't.

But she has always been so supportive of whatever I wanted to do so she wrote my name on a note which read, *My son is in a wheelchair. He can crawl and he can walk with a walker, and he wants to go out for the wrestling team. I want you to know he is very intelligent and he really wants to do this, but the decision is yours.*

I spoke with the Athletic Director and showed him the pamphlet. He listened, but didn't share my enthusiasm, and more or less brushed it off, most likely thinking I wouldn't pursue it. He mentioned other sports for which I could try out which he felt were a better fit for me. But I told him, "No," I wanted to wrestle.

I'm glad I pushed back because when I spoke with the team's Coach Liu, he told me if I could pass the physical, he'd be happy to have me on his team. I was excited he was so open-minded and caring. I had a chance!

I went to my doctor for a physical and he signed the papers saying I was fit to wrestle. Mom agreed and said she would support me any way she could. I felt powerful despite my disabilities. I wouldn't let it beat me. I was on my way.

Fortunately for me, I found out you don't try out for the wrestling team as you do in many other sports. You're on the team until you quit. When you practice, you may be up against older, stronger, and faster upperclassmen teammates who are in your weight class. What a challenge it was for someone like me who had never wrestled, much less someone with my physical disabilities. *Had I made the right decision?*

But being on the team doesn't mean you'll automatically get to wrestle in a match, either. Only the top ones in each weight class get the opportunity. You can sign up for the team, but it's the practices that weed out those who won't make it. They're brutal.

The old line coaches pride themselves on how difficult they can make their practices. I heard of one coach at another school who admitted that at the beginning of each season, he'd keep the team practicing each day until someone quit. That's how he pared his teams down to a manageable number-a pretty tough tactic, but also an effective one. Only the strong survived. *Was I strong enough?*

Our practices were very difficult and brutal compared to many other sports. We trained in a small, dimly lit, smelly, crowded room, complete with a flickering overhead fluorescent light. We had to cope with the heat, where the practice facility's temperature is maintained at an often unbearable 85 to 90 degrees. It was nasty.

The heat, resulting in profuse sweating, helps you control your weight so you can stay in your weight class but challenges you to increase your strength. As a result, most wrestlers are lean, mean, fighting machines. *Could I make it through?* It wasn't glamorous for sure, but I was all in.

I quickly learned that wrestlers aren't like most other people. Their intensity is at a much higher level. You must be a force to survive in that type of environment. And you must work hard because thirty or more guys are going out for the team.

On none of my high school teams did everyone that started a season stay on the team, and I was the only one with physical disabilities. But despite my obstacles, I learned at an early age that attitude is everything. *I can do this! I will do this!*

During the first few days of practice, I could tell the other guys on the team and the coaches were hesitant to physically engage with me as they normally would another. For sure, they had never experienced anyone like me before. I think they wondered about my physical condition and ability. *Can he work out? Would he get hurt?*

During the first couple of weeks, Coach wouldn't let me practice with the team. I had to wait until they were finished. At the end when they were gone, he would help me out of my wheelchair and work with me, one on one.

He wanted to see for himself what I could do – to understand my capabilities. I understood his thinking. I was so different than the average wrestler, and with me also came special challenges. But I didn't like being separated from the rest of the team.

Soon I got up enough courage to tell him I wanted to work out with the team because I didn't want to be excluded. He thought about it and replied, "Okay, we can do that," and from that point on, I worked out with the team. I was starting to feel I belonged.

However, even though he allowed me to do drills and wrestle with them, most of the team wasn't very comfortable practicing with me. They needed to get used to interacting with me. But after all my years of physical therapy, I was probably in better shape than they realized. No one wanted to be the guy to hurt me – the kid in the wheelchair. So I encouraged them to *bring it on* because I was going to *bring it* to them.

My challenge was way over the top for a person in my situation, but it helped relieve any hesitancy they had toward going all out against me, and it motivated me as well because I had to back up my challenge. But I knew a statement like that from a cocky freshman probably meant I was setting myself up for a rough time. So be it. I could handle it.

The key attributes of a good wrestler are skill, knowledge, determination, and heart. This was my kind of sport. I was ready. *Bring it on!*

At first, it was exciting for me to be on a real team, but there were times early on when I questioned my decision to wrestle. While I loved the camaraderie and being accepted by the team, the practices were often overwhelming to me. I could see the coaches were trying to separate the men from the boys, a natural elimination process, but it was doubly hard for me just to keep up.

In those early practices, we did a drill where the team ran wind sprints up and down the mat for conditioning, but I had to crawl since I couldn't run. What a sight that must have been. My teammates must have been scratching their heads wondering how long I'd last. The first few times I tried, I couldn't even make it all the way down the mat. My lungs were burning, my arms were tired - I was gassed, as you would expect.

I started to doubt my decision to pursue wrestling because as strong as my desire was to do it, I wasn't sure my body could perform to the levels required for such a grueling and demanding sport.

With all my self-doubts dominating my thoughts, and me considering throwing in the towel, what helped me push through it was when Coach Liu, who must have seen me struggling, confided that he wasn't going to give up on me if I didn't give up on him. He said we were going to fight through and overcome my obstacles together.

His statement and encouragement helped me through this immensely difficult time. It reminded me that to succeed you have to surround yourself with positive, encouraging people. And it taught me to look to others to help overcome obstacles in my life, and not to feel we have to shoulder the burden alone. Just as important, it also told me he looked at me as one of his kids and wasn't going to give up on me just because I was in a wheelchair with physical challenges.

That meant the world to me because he could have just as easily pulled me aside and told me I had given it a good try but wrestling just wasn't for me, and I didn't have anything to be ashamed of for quitting.

Had he not said and done what he did when he did, I don't know how I may have reacted in a moment of exhaustion and frustration. I may have quit had he urged me to do so. But no, instead he gave me hope and encouragement at a very bleak time for me.

Sometimes I wonder if I may have presented him with a coaching challenge which he wanted to overcome as well. What a great coach he was.

Another time we were enduring a very difficult practice and everyone was tired and struggling. We had so many guys on the team that when we ran up and down the mat we needed to go off in singles, followed by pairs.

It was very hard for me because I had to keep crawling up and down the mat, much more difficult for me than the others who were running. One time I took a break and didn't go down the line when it was my turn because I didn't think Coach was paying attention to me, as he appeared highly focused on the other guys.

At the end of practice, he came over and asked me why I didn't crawl as I should have when I skipped. He told me to believe him when he told me I was important to him.

Though I was embarrassed, it buoyed my spirits to know he was as focused on me as he was everyone else and I wasn't just a "special" kid in a wheelchair who was a team member in name only. He considered me one of the guys and wanted me to succeed, and it helped keep me going.

Through it all, I learned wrestling is a lot about simply surviving, and I was trying my hardest to do just that. Technique and style are important, but it is also a mental attitude where you must possess the primal tendencies of instinct and survival. You must approach the mat as if you're going to be battling for your next breath.

While those early practices were intentionally hard to eliminate those who weren't mentally tough enough, they were also for physical conditioning.

Conditioning is important in every sport for both strength and stamina. In wrestling, you have to be in great shape because as you tire, you will lose your form and technique and fall back into bad habits. It's a natural reaction to fatigue.

But in a wrestling match, you can't signal to the coach to take you out for a breather. You're on the mat until your match is over. No one wants to lose because they aren't in shape.

I think the training was also as much mental as it was physical. You must have the right mindset and attitude to work through it. It's a marathon, not a sprint. Proceed accordingly. Pace yourself.

I believe my intensity about the physical therapy I endured from a young age played a big role in molding me for the rigorous wrestling training regimen. So maybe I'd actually been training for this moment my whole life.

Whatever your hand finds to do, do it with all your might.
—Ecclesiastes 9:10

***

Brenda:

When I took Willie to Fairdale High to enroll as a freshman and he saw the wrestling pamphlet and said he wanted to wrestle, I thought, *oh boy*. I had seen him go through so many disappointments in his life because of his physical limitations that my first reaction was, "Oh God, I don't want to see him suffer through more."

I didn't know what being on a high school wrestling team even entailed, but a mother's instinct is to protect her child, especially from the unknown. But Willie was so insistent that he wanted to wrestle that I went ahead and wrote a note to the coach for him. Lo and behold he ends up on the team and it changed his life forever. I'm glad I listened to and trusted him.

He's always been very competitive, so I wasn't totally surprised he wanted to wrestle. As a kid, he enjoyed watching anything on TV which was sports related. It could have been water polo or any sport, it didn't matter. Even before he probably understood the meaning of sports and athletic competition, as a baby, whenever a sporting event on TV went to a commercial, he would cry because he wanted to watch the competition so badly.

As he got older, once when I was doing laundry while he was watching TV, he was yelling and screaming, so I rushed to him to see what all the fuss was about. It turns out he was totally engrossed in a sumo wrestling match.

He said, "Mom, I'm rooting for the guy wearing the purple towel." When he eventually lost the match he said, "Well, now I'm rooting for the guy in the blue towel." He loved watching the competition and I knew he now understood the difference between winning and losing, not just competing.

His fascination with physical activity may have started as early as one year old. Because of the debilitating effects of cerebral palsy, he wasn't able to roll over until his first birthday. But once he did, he immediately began commando crawling in which he pulled himself around on his stomach and kept crawling back and forth across our kitchen floor. When he was older, he was able to rise up on his hands and knees and crawl like others. Then he could really zip around!

I believe the physical demands facing him in his life are what piqued his interest in sports as well as his desire to compete against others.

When he was young, he was in a T-ball league for kids in wheelchairs. He got bored when he was on the field because it seemed like the organizers were excited just to see the kids hit the ball. And while it may have been an accomplishment for some, getting pushed to first base, then to second, and so on, wasn't for him. He needed excitement – competition! He was always competitive and wanted to beat whomever or whatever he was up against. He didn't want anyone pushing him around the bases in a wheelchair.

He tried wheelchair basketball for a while. And it was pretty competitive. But he wasn't very good at it, so it was boring unless he was faced with a competitive situation.

Once, he generated a basketball challenge and succeeded. He had a good friend, Genc, who was from Kosovo. As a baby, he lost his lower legs to frostbite, and as a result, is a double amputee. But he was an excellent athlete, a natural.

He often wore prosthetic legs but was good at basketball, softball or anything he played. I was always amazed at what he could do and I know he inspired Willie as an example of someone who could overcome anything if he put his mind to it. Willie said he often thought about Genc when he faced his many obstacles in wrestling.

Willie and Genc were hanging out together in their wheelchairs at a local playground and two kids came by and asked them if they wanted to play basketball. Willie replied, "Yes," so he and Genc pushed themselves up to the basketball court.

When they arrived, the other two kids asked how they should make up the teams. They wondered how to split them up since they were both in wheelchairs, and one should be on each team.

Willie said he and Genc would take them on. The other two said they didn't want to play against two kids in wheelchairs, but Willie insisted. So they played, and he and Genc beat them! When Willie came home, he was so excited and proud of his challenge and their accomplishment. Some friendly competition will often bring out the best in people.

His love of sports was self-originated because he didn't grow up around anyone else who enjoyed or participated in them, so he wasn't indoctrinated into sports by an older sibling or family member.

I never was a sports nut like him. His father and I were amateur musicians, not sports fanatics, and our passion was leading Praise and Worship at Church for many years. We took great pride in our roles and accomplishments there and our mission filled us up, so we weren't looking for other interests like sports. That wasn't the case for Willie.

I don't know what all his thoughts were when he wanted to get into wrestling. It was a big first step for him, but he was brave enough to try it. Did he think he would just be on the team and not be able to wrestle in the matches but would be able to work out and learn the sport? Maybe, and that may have satisfied him. But that's not the way it played out, fortunately.

Little did I know at the time, how sports, especially wrestling, would later come to play such a big role in Willie's life. And how could I know that even when he began, he would attract local attention? In his first year a local Louisville TV station, WLKY came by to shoot video of him practicing. I suppose a kid with cerebral palsy wrestling is a special interest story. Looking back, I wonder if that type of attention put unnecessary pressure on him to succeed.

But if it did, he rose to the occasion. As a freshman, he had to adapt to a new school, new friends and a new system. He was a member of a team in a sport in which he had no prior experience and his coaches and teammates had no previous experience with a team member like him. Everyone had to adjust to each other, and they did. He endured the physically demanding practices and never complained, not knowing where they would take him.

But he leaped into wrestling head first, consistent with his personality. He took all he could from the experience but gave back so much more. He was a champion from the start.

2

My Birth and Adoption—
In the Lord's Hands

*As you do not know the path of the wind, or how
the body is formed in a mother's womb, so you cannot
understand the work of God, the Maker of all things.*
—Ecclesiastes 11:5

Willie:

If I had to sum up my life to this point in a single sentence, I'm not sure I would know what to say. How did I come to be a wrestler with CP? Well, it started before I was born - my life didn't get off to a normal start. It would be hard to describe almost anything in my life as being normal.

But each of our lives is our own, start to finish. My adoptive mother, Brenda, often spoke to me about my birth and adoption because my very inquisitive young mind wanted to know all the details. I believe she enjoyed recounting it as many times as she did because it is a very unique and complicated story. And I believe it reinforced her faith and trust in God, which is still important to her today, as it is to me.

I was born on September 23rd, 1995 in Louisville, Kentucky. How I came to be with the Burtons is quite a tale. As the story goes, Brenda and my adoptive father, Larry, were members of a small local church called Churchman Chapel. Another church member had previously adopted a baby through the Church. The girl who had given up her baby in that instance knew another girl who said she felt it was the best thing for her to do, too. She was told by her friend, "Well, I contacted this Church and someone in the congregation adopted my baby."

The young girl then contacted the Church and spoke with Mike Duke, the pastor. She was a seventeen-year-old named Trina Jones who already had a two-year-old child. Trina was my birth mother. She asked Pastor Mike if he would inquire of his congregation to see if anyone would be willing to adopt her baby too because she didn't want to have an abortion. He shared her story with his congregation the following Sunday and asked them to pray for the woman and her unborn baby.

Brenda:

I was a member of the congregation and heard her story. The following day I was sitting down to read my Bible and it fell open to the story of Abraham and Sarah in Genesis. A scripture passage seemed to jump from the page. It read, "And you, Sarah, shall have a son."

The words of the verse shocked me since I was not able to have children, as much as how I came to read it. It brought to mind other Bible passages where God said he would bless a childless woman with children.

I shouted, "Oh my God!" Larry, my husband inquired, "What?" I said, "Larry, I think we're supposed to take the baby." We were both surprised by my announcement because, by our own admission, we disliked children probably more than anyone else in our Church.

We were both in our early forties at the time, had been married eight years, had no children, and weren't looking to fill a void in our lives. We both knew we weren't very patient with young children. In fact, Larry often professed he didn't even like kids. We were perhaps the most unlikely candidates in the Church to adopt a child, much less a newborn.

Coincidentally, Pastor Duke called us shortly thereafter and said, "Do you remember the baby we prayed for yesterday?

Would you two pray that whoever is supposed to take it lets me know soon?" We said, yes, and sat down to pray about it, and then left to run some errands.

While we were gone, it seemed everywhere we went we kept seeing the same sign on various billboards which we had never noticed before. It contained a verse from Jeremiah 1:5, which reads, "I knew you before you were formed in your mother's womb." The meaning of the verse is that God knows a person's purpose on this earth before they are born.

Again, one billboard after another proclaimed the same message. We thought it almost spooky to have seen so many we had never seen before. Was God sending us a message?

My head was spinning from all the signs and thoughts we were having about us having a child. It was exciting though to think we were following God's will.

When we returned from our errands, I called Pastor Duke and boldly announced, "Mike, Larry and I will take that baby." Mike laughed when he heard my statement and said, "I knew it was you." I asked how he was so certain.

He replied that earlier in the day he was thinking about the baby and said, "Lord, we've got six kids of our own, what's one more? We'll take that baby." And the Lord spoke to him in his thoughts and said, "It's Larry's and Brenda's baby."

Kathy Duke, Mike's wife also told us their daughter, Faye came home from school and said, "Mom, I've been thinking all day about Larry and Brenda and how they should take that baby." It confirmed to Kathy what she had already been mulling over in her mind that we should adopt the new baby and she spoke with Mike about it. In my mind, Willie was destined to be with us, no doubt about it and the Dukes would become his second family.

Our decision to adopt the baby was a big surprise to almost everyone who knew us, but they didn't know God had His own plan. Little did we know what lay ahead for us, and Willie.

***

I was a nurse, so I wanted to meet the expectant mother to learn her medical history. Kathy said Trina wanted to meet us as well, so we went to the hospital to visit her. She was being treated for problems with early contractions, which the doctors were trying to stop since she was only 7 ½ months pregnant.

I asked her medical and lifestyle questions, including if she knew who the baby's father was, as well as if she had ever used drugs. She named the father and replied that she had never taken drugs.

Kathy and I stepped from Trina's room into the hall because the nurses were giving her Brethene shots to delay her preterm labor. The doctors hoped it would allow time to administer her steroid injections to help the baby's lungs mature, for they feared he was going to be born before his lungs were sufficiently developed, which would significantly decrease his chances of survival.

We were praying that his oxygen would be at the desired levels if he was born early, which is a common problem with premature births. The doctor approached and asked one of the nurses if she knew the breathing counts. The nurse gave him the numbers and he replied, "It's not possible they're that good."

Kathy and I smiled, looked at each other and said, "With God, anything is possible."

After four hours we left the hospital expecting the baby wouldn't be born for a couple more months, but at 2:00 a.m. the next morning our phone rang and we heard Kathy say, "Your son is here." Trina's contractions had returned soon after we left the hospital the previous evening and the doctors couldn't get them to stop, so he was born, all 2 ½ pounds of him.

***

Willie:

Here I was, new to the world, in the Intensive Care Unit of Kosair Hospital, fighting for my life, had no name, and was probably going to be adopted by folks who didn't care for kids - but then my life got harder. Trina lied - she had used drugs while she was pregnant. She actually was addicted to crack cocaine, so I was born addicted, myself.

I was, what is commonly referred to as a "crack baby," and my condition initially went undiagnosed as the doctors didn't know of her drug use. Everyone wondered why I was always crying. After some tests they had their answer - I was going through drug withdrawal.

The doctors asked Brenda if she knew if Trina had used drugs while she was pregnant, but all she could tell them was Trina told her, "no." So in addition to being born prematurely, fighting to maintain a normal body temperature and nutrition and all the other complications that go with being a premie, I had to cope with agonizing drug withdrawal symptoms. What a horrible process for a newborn to suffer through.

Then things got even worse. About two weeks after I was born the doctors diagnosed a hemorrhage in the left side of my brain, an event which often occurs in premature babies. The brains of those babies aren't fully developed and are more susceptible to problems than if they are carried full term. Had Trina not taken drugs, there is a strong probability I would have been carried full-term and not have suffered the hemorrhage, but I for sure wouldn't have been born addicted to drugs, had she led a better lifestyle.

The doctors soon met Brenda and Larry at my incubator and told them they may want to reconsider my adoption, on account of the hemorrhage. It had seriously affected my legs and right arm and hand. It is hard to diagnose the extent of the damage in a newborn, but their experience told them I most likely would be confined to a wheelchair, and with all the other challenges confronting me, my prognosis was not very good.

As I laid in the intensive care unit fighting for my life, I was stuck between two worlds. My birth parents were out of the picture, and my prospective adoptive ones were being advised to reconsider their decision and walk away. *What would happen to me? Would I become a ward of the state and end up who knows where?*

Fortunately for me, kind and caring people were dealing with my circumstances especially Our Lord who may have wondered if He shouldn't have hit the "back" button a few times. But He has dealt with much worse situations than mine and He would take care of me.

Brenda:

On hearing the bad news, I shuddered but gathered myself and walked into the hall. I leaned against the wall and thought, "Lord, if this child is going to run and jump and skip and play and be totally normal someday, I'm asking You to give me a sign and have the nurses dress him in a green outfit tomorrow." In the Old Testament, they called this laying out a fleece before God in prayer, asking Him for a sign to prove that this is truly His will.

Larry and I drove back to the hospital the next morning and I fretted about what may await us there. I had asked the Lord for a sign that this little baby would be able to lead a normal life. *Had he listened? How could I be sure? If He decided to send me a sign some other way, how would I know?* I placed my trust in Him. *Was that enough?* I prayed it was.

While we rode the elevator up to the newborn intensive care unit I stared at the floor, lost in my thoughts. *Had we made a mistake? Would we be good parents? What would we do if we weren't given a sign? How could we just walk away?* When I held that precious baby for the first time he was so tiny, but I felt a bond between us. He needed me and maybe I needed him.

My head swirled with doubts as the doors opened and I stepped off the elevator and we proceeded down the hall to the NICU. As we approached the door I hesitated, knowing I may be faced with one of the most critical decisions of my life. We scrubbed in and put on our gowns and as we entered and I looked at Willie, my heart soared. He was dressed in a bright green knitted outfit, one I had never seen him dressed in before or after that day. I had my answer - the Lord had spoken. We had a baby. I was going to be a mom!

The Lord appeared to have given us divine direction, but then almost immediately the doctors announced Willie most likely had little or no cognitive ability and would probably live his life in a vegetative state. What a shock! Larry's and my confidence wavered and we reached a point where we thought we wouldn't be able to manage this burden emotionally or financially and seriously considered canceling the adoption proceedings. But somehow God in His power had a most unusual way of turning things around. He must have decided Willie was going to be our son.

Our attorney soon called from the hospital and said he heard we were considering dropping the adoption. We replied that we were because the doctors didn't give Willie a very good prognosis - a horrible one, in fact. Thankfully, a nurse got on the phone and said, "I hate it when that doctor talks to parents because he usually upsets them, and your son is not going to be a vegetable."

The circumstances had an unusual way of getting turned around and the nurse's words changed our minds. Willie was back into our lives. Was the Lord just testing us? Willie would often tease us that we tried to get rid of him, but he came back. We always laughed and agreed. The Lord does work in mysterious ways. Willie's proof!

***

Willie:

I love the story of my adoption because my new parents both acted out of faith and I know God had a hand in choosing who would adopt me and take me in as their own.

After being in the hospital for two months, my new mom and dad took me into their hearts and brought me home. Brenda and Larry were now Mommy and Daddy and they loved me and cared for me as if I was their own.

I had filled out from my birth weight of 2 ½ pounds to a robust 6 pounds, 2 ½ ounces and it was time for me to leave, despite all my other medical conditions. For all they told me I went through from my birth, I must have had a legion of angels looking after me, and I'm sure they followed me to my new home with the Burtons.

They named me William after my dad, Larry, whose real name is William, and his father, William. Everyone called me Willie, though. I think I'll always be called Willie, although Dad often calls me Spuds because he claims when he first held me I was so small I wasn't any bigger than a bag of potato spuds.

A new baby with special needs must have been a major adjustment for my parents, given their age and their never having cared for an infant. In fact, when they were considering my adoption, Mom, ever the planner, prayed and said, "Lord, if you're going to send us this baby, Larry is going to have to bring it up." Her meaning was that her work schedule as a nurse was often long and wasn't as predictable as his as a pipefitter in the maintenance division at the University of Louisville.

After they brought me home, since Mom was making more money as an orthopedic neurology (ortho-neuro) nurse than Dad, and he had a lot of accrued vacation time, so initially, he used the Family Medical Leave Act to stay home and care for me. He was Mr. Mom and his new challenge was monitoring my breathing with a machine because of my underdeveloped lungs. It was a big suitcase-sized apparatus with an alarm system that sounded if I stopped breathing, which happened regularly. My brain would go to sleep and simply forget to breathe.

Dad said I was home only a few days and he and I were alone once when the alarm sounded. The hospital staff gave him instructions to shake me to startle me so I would wake up and take a deep breath. Terrified that he was home alone with me and my nurse mother was away at work, he shook me as instructed, and I woke up. I immediately began screaming because he had startled me and the sound of the alarm was very piercing and unsettling, which frightened both of us.

It was a long process to get the alarm to stop sounding once it went off. He began going through a series of sequential button-pushing movements to silence it. He said he was so nervous it took what seemed like an eternity to shut it off. After a month or so the steps became routine, so he was able to easily wake me to start breathing, as well as shut off the alarm. He had it down to a science.

At home, I was still battling the effects of withdrawal from the drugs my birth mother used while she was pregnant with me. Mom and Dad thought I had colic because if I wasn't sleeping, or didn't have a bottle or a pacifier in my mouth, I was crying. Dad said one day he was sitting alone thinking about my incessant, heart-breaking crying. Though I was a tiny lion, I had a mighty roar.

He must have neared his breaking point because he went and got some blankets, laid them on the living room carpet and placed me on them so I wouldn't get hurt. He went outside and stood in the snow and watched me through the picture window of our home where he could see but not hear me. He needed a break from my crying.

He has since told me he could understand how parents who were strung out on drugs or alcohol could harm a child who wouldn't stop crying. Obviously, it was a challenge for him, but he found a way to cope until my withdrawal eased and I began acting more like a normal baby.

***

After Dad had gone through all of his paid time off and returned to work, I stayed with the Dukes all day. Mike and Kathy had six children and she was homeschooling them when I was born. It was a very interesting situation, and a blessing, because they had considered adopting me and now they were having a great influence on my upbringing.

Mike, as Pastor of the Church, had gotten many calls during his twenty-three years there from those wishing to give up their babies for adoption. They were pleased when I was placed with a couple in their Church who they knew so well.

But I also think Mike and Kathy Duke felt they had a vested interest in me since they had encouraged and participated in arranging my adoption. They may have wondered too, at times, if they had done the right thing by the Burtons, given my physical limitations.

Their children were also happy when the Burtons adopted me because with the two families being so close, they got to share me. When I was young, every little thing I did they made a fuss over and celebrated it. Their treatment of me was a tremendous boost to my self-confidence.

Others should be so lucky to be surrounded by such a loving, supportive family. I think they are the reason I was and still am happy all the time. I didn't have to struggle with rejection – I was always well loved.

The youngest in their family, Timothy, was also born with a mild case of cerebral palsy, so their family was already oriented to a special needs child. In fact, we both had physical therapy with the same therapist and would go for treatments together.

Based on the odds for improvement the doctors gave me, I shouldn't have been able to do half of what I've done, and I owe a lot of it to the Dukes. I surpassed most all the expectations others had for me at the time.

Dad and I spent a lot of time together while I was an infant and a toddler. While he had a reputation of not liking kids, I must have changed his opinion. He said he started to enjoy me, as most parents do, when I started to develop a personality.

I had thick curly hair and in Dad's words, I was as cute as a button, and he loved it. He'd take me to Kroger's supermarket and the women there would be fawning over me telling him how much I looked like him. It was funny since I was adopted. Dad and I remained close which was good, given the challenges which laid ahead for me.

Brenda:
Psalm 113 says, "I will bless the childless woman with children." Before Willie came into our lives I used to read those words and think *Lord, do you mean that literally?* I was happy in my life at the time, so I didn't give it much thought.

There is so much more in a walk with God than most Christians know. Larry and I were in a Bible study session two years before Willie was born and a man there prophesized over me that the Lord was going to bless me with a child. I had forgotten about his prophecy until Willie entered our lives. Willie loved this story when I would repeat it because he felt his coming to us fulfilled a prophecy.

When we were presented with the decision to adopt, I was afraid I wouldn't be a good mom since I had never prepared myself to be a mother. The first time I held Willie was on the first day he was born, a two-and-a-half-pound baby boy. I thought, *oh God*, I dread the thought of having to potty train you. I thought that was going to be one of the hardest things I'd face. Little did I know what was to come and that potty training would be one of the easiest.

I know the birth of any baby is considered a miracle itself - one of life's blessings. The birth and survival of such a tiny premature baby with a brain bleed which caused his cerebral palsy and who was also addicted to crack cocaine - now that's a real miracle, in my opinion. If the Lord saw it fit to let him live, we could surely raise him in His glory. It was my faith which got me through all the upcoming challenges I would face.

The Dukes are a special family and were lifesavers to us when it came to raising Willie. Each workday Larry or I would take Willie to their home early in the morning and he would be there until nearly 6:00 p.m. when one of us would pick him up. This went on for years. Kathy also homeschooled Willie with her own children when he was in kindergarten and first grade.

As a nurse, I took care of most of Willie's physical needs, but Kathy was like his everyday mom since she spent so much time with him. She treated him like he was her own. She threw him birthday parties, and did other special things for him and would take him places with her own children despite him needing special attention. She was a loving caregiver. Willie couldn't have asked for a better situation – two moms and instant brothers and sisters!

And now these three remain faith, hope,
and love. But the greatest of these is love.
—*I Corinthians 13:13*

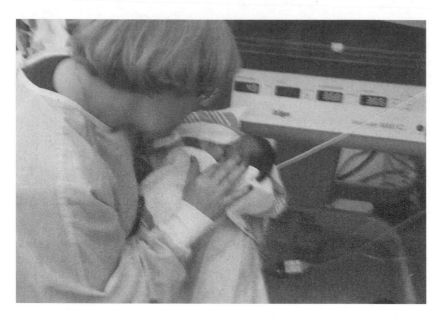

My baby boy.

3

The Competitions—
Hard Lessons to Learn

But as for you, be strong and do not give up,
for your work will be rewarded.
—*Chronicles 15:7*

Willie:
Other than being rescued from an almost certain existence of misery and despair by being adopted by the Burtons, becoming a wrestler may be my biggest and most unlikely life-changing event to date. It both changed and opened up my life, most unexpectedly, and like many of the other situations I have faced began in a most unlikely way.

My wrestling in matches began immediately in my freshman year. On weekends we competed in multi-team tournaments, but on every Wednesday night, we usually competed against just one other team.

I was nervous the whole week leading up to my first match. I was inexperienced and had never been in a match and though I practiced against my teammates, matches are where it counts.

We didn't know my true weight class because it was difficult to accurately weigh me since I needed assistance to stand on the scale, which distorted my true weight reading. The referees looked at the scale but then usually made an educated guess at my true weight.

When the season was about to begin, the coaches asked me if I wanted to wrestle-off in practice against a teammate in the 120-pound weight class to qualify me to wrestle in the match, and I agreed. I was overmatched, so I lost.

On the night of the matches, against Doss High School, the coaches spoke with me and said I probably didn't weigh 120 pounds and asked if I would consider moving down to the 106-pound class. Again, I agreed. Our coach came back later and told me that with my change in weight class, I'd be wrestling a girl and asked if I was okay with it.

Some teams have girls on them. We didn't have any at the time on our team at Fairdale, but many other schools did, so it wasn't so unusual. Besides, the matches are determined solely by weight class, so your opponent is of similar size and build. I was anxious to get my first match behind me, so I told my coach, "A match is a match, no matter who it's against."

My heart was pounding through my chest as my match time drew near. I wasn't overconfident and couldn't tell if I had a very good chance of winning since I had never competed before. But it was exciting to be on the mat, representing my school, and I wanted very much to make a strong showing, to feel I belonged, and if I won, to strut my stuff!

Soon it was my turn and my teammates helped me onto the mat. When I began wrestling in practice I'd get up on my knees and try to grapple with my opponent as I did this time. It wasn't a good strategy, so the match lasted only twenty seconds and I got pinned. She was more experienced than me and it showed. I was stunned. Not only did I lose, I got smoked!

After the match, when I crawled over to shake hands with her and her coach, she was crying because she felt bad for beating me so easily. That made me feel worse, but I ended up consoling her, telling her not to cry because her beating me would actually help me to improve.

While I was comforting her though I thought, *man, I just lost to a girl. I don't believe it.* It was a wake-up call of sorts for me. Matches were tough and I needed to improve - and fast! It wasn't a good start, for sure.

The loss made me wonder again about my future on the team. Reality can be a cruel teacher. I was new to the sport, so I didn't know what to expect. I thought, *wow, this is terrible. This is not what I expected. Would I* always be losing for the team, costing us points? *What if I never win?* I thought at the time. *Why am I doing this?*

I was again filled with self-doubts, but my coaches and teammates were very reassuring which helped settle me down. My coaches probably felt bad for sending me out there, to begin with, but we both had to learn what I could do and there was no better time than the present, I suppose.

Wrestling in the 106-pound weight class presented its own challenges. We had no other team members in that weight class so it meant if the coaches sent me out there, I'd be wrestling with the varsity, not the junior varsity as I expected I would. This meant I'd be wrestling more times, not fewer, against older more experienced wrestlers. Who would have figured?

As the season progressed, what probably kept me from quitting was my coaches' continual encouragement: "Okay, you didn't win this weekend, but we'll get you better for next weekend." They never gave up. They believed in me and never stopped believing in me. They always expected me to win the next time out.

With all the time and effort they gave me, how could I give up? I later learned that there had been fully able-bodied wrestlers at Fairdale who didn't win a match until their senior year. Learning this gave me some perspective and helped ease my anxieties, but I certainly hoped I wouldn't share that distinction with the others.

In the beginning, my coaches and teammates would urge me to go out and just survive for the six-minute match, so it wouldn't be six points against our team. They told me our goal was for me to fight as hard as I could, do the best I could and try not to get pinned. I always fought hard and sometimes I'd get pinned and sometimes I didn't. In wrestling scoring, if you pin someone you get six points, and there are many other ways to score points.

Throughout my wrestling career, I had the benefit of winning many matches by forfeit. Often the other team didn't have a wrestler in my low weight class and I'd be granted a win and six points toward our team total. It obviously didn't feel as good as winning a match against another wrestler, but it helped our team, so I was happy to be contributing. Also, when I did wrestle and though I didn't beat anyone head to head, I often did win points in those matches. I didn't get pinned in every match.

While my head-to-head losses continued to mount as the year passed, I gained confidence each time I competed. When I lost, I didn't feel it was the end of the world; that I was an awful wrestler and shouldn't be out there, and therefore should quit. Rather, I would go back to practice and we'd analyze the critical points which triggered my loss in the match.

I needed to learn what moves and strategies I needed to change to increase my chances of winning. I wasn't discouraged because they say you learn more from your losses than your wins. It would have been nice to have been able to test the theory though.

***

After each match, my coaches would not only analyze what transpired but would try to come up with new wrestling techniques to either make use of my skills or to neutralize my opponent's skill or techniques. They even scoured YouTube for some recordings on wrestlers with physical disabilities to learn how each one compensated for their own weaknesses.

My skills *were* different than others. My opponents rarely if ever wrestled someone on their knees, or who even approached them on all fours. But I had no choice. Did that give me an advantage? Probably not, but then again, rarely did anyone in my weight class have my upper body strength. I had to emphasize and take advantage of my own attributes.

However, since I often didn't have the speed and coordination to escape an opponent's hold, my coaches decided to have me start on top, or be leaning over, the other wrestler whenever it came to the choice at the beginning of a period. This is a weaker position from which to begin, but my physical limitations left us no choice.

They also spent many hours working with me to improve my cradle holds where I could use my upper body strength to lock over an opponent if I could maneuver them into the right position. I couldn't push very well with my legs, but I could push some with my knees to try to roll an opponent over. It was a strategy and technique I worked on endlessly to improve.

A benefit of the art of wrestling is that you must engage your opponent. You can't dodge or run from them and earn enough points to win with evasion. You are in constant contact with them. You grapple and you constantly struggle with them, which gives you an opportunity to look for opportunities to exploit your skills over them. You obviously know your skills better than your opponent does. It's a lot like life, in general. You learn about others, and you learn about yourself. Even with my upper body strength advantage, it took me a long time to be able to use it to win a match; too long.

In my junior year one of our coaches, Joe Jarvis, began spending more of his time with me, working on my techniques. Before, I waited for my opponent to step in toward me, and then I sprung toward their legs at a low angle. If I got overextended, I'd be off-balance and would get rolled over, which happened to me frequently. If I dove and missed, they could quickly circle around behind me and jump on my back. Or they would hop back out in front and turn me. Coach was just trying to minimize some of my small mistakes that were costing me in my matches.

He suggested I should instead wait to spring toward my opponent until they were moving toward me. It would shorten the gap between us, so I wouldn't be so off-balance from being overextended.

All my coaches worked with me constantly to get in and stay close to my opponents. It was important for me to take advantage of my upper body strength and my strong left-hand grip to counteract my opponents' attempts to take advantage of their skills over me. If I got overextended, I lost leverage and couldn't pull them toward me.

He also instituted a couple of drills for me to practice. One was to crawl on my hands and knees, while someone else pushed or pulled on me, which helped strengthen my legs. Another was to have someone push on one of my hips, or pull me from either side, to knock me off balance. It caused me to focus on not being pushed over, which happened to me in many of my matches.

Coach was trying to get my center of gravity below me and improve my balance, so I wasn't falling over as often, which was a big problem I needed to overcome. We practiced these drills and moves constantly and I felt I was becoming a better wrestler, despite not yet having won a match.

It was a great challenge for my coaches to come up with new ways to help me improve because of my physical limitations, which dictated my moves and holds. But they never gave up looking for better ways to cope with what we had to deal with.

Due to my lack of mobility and the challenge of maintaining my center of gravity, I couldn't turn very fast to react to an opponent's moves or to initiate my own. Since my right hand is not very strong and I don't have full use of it, I can't grip normally which requires me to alter my grip to be able to hold onto someone.

Kyle Maynard, the well-known disabled wrestler in Georgia, noted in his memoir that a wrestler must have strong neck muscles to be successful. He's right. Your opponent's objective is to roll you on your back, so they have a much better chance of pinning you and winning the match.

In wrestling, your head and neck primarily control your body's movement, so if your opponent is able to turn your neck over to one side, your body will follow. If you have a strong neck and can keep your head from turning, your opponent will have a much more difficult time rolling you over. A weaker neck will allow you to be turned easier. If he controls your head, he controls your body. Strong neck muscles are so important.

I worked on improving my neck strength as much as anyone on the team because I was more susceptible to being turned because of my lack of balance and weak hips. Those deficiencies allowed my opponents to roll me over more easily.

But the many issues I had to cope with when I wrestled were not only physical but strategic as well. If I hadn't lost a match in the first period and was able to get to the second, what would be my strategy for the remainder of my match? If I was down, what moves could I use to escape and not be pinned?

I couldn't stand so that wasn't a viable option, so our strategy needed to be based more on moves from down on the mat. I couldn't rise up and hit a switch move to gain a stronger position from a neutral one against an opponent because you must move your hands and feet at the same time to execute it properly. So my coaches came up with a few moves they felt would work but needed to be tweaked a bit to suit me so I could execute a roll on an opponent.

These were many of the challenges my coaches coped with to help me improve and win. It was outstanding how they spent so much time and effort and took so much personal interest in me. They could have parked me in a corner, consoling me by telling me I'm trying my best and that's good enough, which would have allowed them to spend more time with the rest of the team where there obviously was more upside. But they didn't. Their actions told me I was part of the team as much as anyone else was.

I'd often discussed with Mom and Dad how, had I gone to a different school, the coaches there may not have allowed me to wrestle at all, much less have worked with me as much as the Fairdale coaches did. Think of how my life would have been affected. Our Lord was truly watching out for me, and exercised His will through these great men.

Brenda:

I'm not a sports enthusiast, but I was interested in Willie's wrestling because it meant so much to him and was good for his mental well-being. It was the first time he had ever been on a team, much less a sports team, and it helped his self-confidence which is extremely important in a young person with disabilities.

He must have been pleased, yet surprised when his coaches put him in the first matches, which could be compared to being thrown in the deep end of the pool. He was shocked by the results, yet he didn't back down and he kept working to improve.

Looking back, it was probably the best thing that could have happened to him. His coaches must have had an uncanny ability to know the right thing to do at the time.

I wasn't able to attend many of his matches due to my work schedule, but Larry tried to make as many as he could. But honestly, I found the team matches somewhat boring at times, so I wasn't disappointed in missing many of them. A match would end and there would be some time before the next one began. You'd spend a lot of time sitting in the bleachers in the gym waiting.

Also, I didn't know all the technical details of wrestling, so it was probably less interesting to me than others. But I was there to support Willie. I suppose if I had grown up with wrestling, I would have felt differently, but here in Kentucky, basketball, which is a much faster-paced sport, is king.

Since I didn't make many matches, I didn't know that Willie was having trouble beating an opponent on the mat. He'd come home and if it was a multi-team event, he'd say, "I won one and lost one," which in reality meant he won one on a forfeit because one team didn't have a wrestler in his weight class and he lost to the team who did. He conveniently left out those details.

I can understand his pride causing him not to tell the whole story. He was winning points for his team with the forfeits. Larry and I both wish we had known the real story though and supported him even more. We both thought he was doing great. We may have been able to help him better deal with the disappointment of losing. It was one of his best-kept secrets. But while he had to be humble to deal with his disability, he also needed to be proud to be able to chase his dreams.

4

What is Cerebral Palsy?

For you created my inmost being; you knit me
together in my mother's womb. I praise you because I am
fearfully and wonderfully made; your works are wonderful,
I know that full well.
—Psalms 139:13-14

Willie:
I was diagnosed shortly after my birth with cerebral palsy.
The medical definition of cerebral palsy is that it is a neurological
disorder in which there is loss or impairment of motor function
caused by a non-progressive brain injury or malformation that
occurs while a child's brain is under development. Knowing the
formal definition doesn't make it any easier to cope with though.

Cerebral palsy is commonly referred to as CP. The brain
damage is caused by a brain injury or abnormal development of
the brain which occurs while a child's brain is still developing –
before birth, during birth, or immediately after birth. It primarily
affects body movement, muscle control, coordination, tone,
reflex, posture, and balance. It can also affect your motor skills as
well as your speech.

I have experienced most, if not all, of these symptoms.
They're horrible and can get better or worse as time passes and
our bodies grow and develop. Although the condition itself can

be defined, having cerebral palsy does not define the person who has the condition. I refused to let it define me.

Doctors and others once thought that CP was caused by complications during the birthing process since a baby's head can absorb a lot of stress as it moves through the birth canal. While this does sometimes happen, it's not as common as they once thought. They now think that the majority of cases are caused before the baby is born but by many different sources. My CP was most likely caused by my birth mother's drug abuse prior to my birth. At two and a half pounds I probably didn't have much trouble sliding down the birth canal into the world.

Since CP is also not a genetic birth defect, it's not inherited from one or both parents, so it can affect everyone uniquely and in lots of different areas on one's body.

The bottom line is CP affects muscles and a person's ability to control them. Our muscles can contract too much, too little, or all at the same time. Our arms and hands can be stiff and forced into painful, awkward positions. At times muscle contractions can make our arms and legs tremble or shake. Simple tasks like walking, sitting, or tying shoes may be difficult for some, while others might have difficulty holding objects in their hands. Some people with CP may suffer from intellectual problems, seizures, and vision or hearing impairment. Having been around other people with CP for as long as I have, I've seen or experienced most all of these symptoms.

It's rare to find another person with CP identical to yourself since each case of CP is unique to the individual affected. It also makes it challenging for a person with CP and their caregivers. One person may be totally paralyzed and require constant care, while someone who is partially paralyzed may not need much assistance.

Care can also depend on when and the type of injury occurred. Since CP is damage to the brain that cannot currently be repaired, treatment and therapy is the only thing that helps. There are times when the brain can be somewhat re-trained to lessen some of the effects, and some surgeries can help too.

That's how the doctors and others define CP. But no matter what you call it, it stinks! It's like getting dealt a bad hand in a card game, but you can't throw in or fold, you have to play it – and it lasts a lifetime!

My biggest challenge is my legs which were the most severely affected. They've never ever been strong enough to support my weight, no matter what my age. The entire right side of my body is weaker than the left by comparison, most noticeably in my arm and hand.

For years my hand was knotted in a ball, but back surgery helped alleviate much of the condition. I have had vision issues, not being able to follow words across a page when reading, but a big obstacle for me to overcome is a speech impediment - I stutter. I struggle to overcome it, but it's difficult to master. Communication is so important and unfortunately, a speech impediment draws more attention to the other conditions caused by CP.

Many of those affected by CP have challenges with daily life issues that others find rather routine, and I'm no exception. When I wake in the morning, I have to think about how to execute something as simple as sitting up and moving my legs over the side of my bed. Then I have to focus on how to negotiate myself into my wheelchair.

I also need help getting dressed, going to the bathroom, and getting in and out of the shower, which must have a seat. I can't drive a car yet, so I need to be driven everywhere I go. I'm dependent on others for assistance each and every day. Ever have an injury and have to be on crutches or in a wheelchair for a short time? It's difficult, isn't it? Try dealing with that your entire life. It's not easy no matter how used to it you are.

When I was at all levels of schooling through high school, I had a personal assistant whom the school district provided, who spent the entire school day with me. He helped me get from one class to the other, writing for me if tests were time-based, with my walker if I was using it, and at lunch and going to the restroom.

I was not an invalid, but in order to function in a fast-paced time-driven world, I needed assistance on many tasks or functions that most others rarely think about. I hate that it's this way, but it's the hand I've been dealt. Overall, CP is a life sentence. If you don't learn how to deal with it, it will consume you.

Mine may be a textbook case of the effects of CP, but the rest of my story is where the similarity ends. Like many others, I refused to allow CP to define me. Striving to overcome its effects is how I made my mark. I wouldn't let it beat me.

Brenda:

Caring for a child with CP is terribly difficult, much more so than I realized when we agreed to adopt Willie. I thought as a nurse I could handle it, but I wasn't prepared for the emotional challenges it presented. As far as the physical aspects like putting Willie in a wheelchair, as an orthopedic nurse, I was used to that. When patients have surgeries or fractures, lifting and moving them around is part of the job.

But the emotional side of things was much different. There were several times when I got angry with God, very angry, and I would admit it to the Lord at the time.

I said, "Lord, you know my heart so I can't hide it from you, but I'm angry with you right now - *really* angry. Why did You choose me for this burden? I have served You well since I've been saved. I've borne witness for You and helped save others. Why is it that those of us who have done so much are asked to do more? This shouldn't be."

Should I have felt blessed or honored that He called on me for this task? In fairness to Him, if things had been different, I probably would have questioned why He hadn't called on me for this duty - He knows I'm His servant and will do as He wishes. But ours is not to question His decisions; ours is to have faith in them.

It's hard to see your son sitting in a wheelchair when there's a group of kids in the neighborhood playing basketball and you can see that *I want to play* look on his face and you know he can't and there's nothing you can do about it.

So many things he wanted to do but couldn't. Simple things like running through the house playing hide and seek, which all kids love to do. We'd do our best to do those things and we'd play hide and seek, but with his being in a wheelchair, there were only two places in the house where he could hide - behind the dining room table and behind my bed.

I'd go through the whole house acting like I was looking for him. But if he was happy, I was happy. He also got a big kick out of me chasing him in his wheelchair through the house with the vacuum cleaner. I don't know what the thrill was with that, but if he got some enjoyment from it, I did it.

He didn't get to go outside as much as other kids but one winter after a snowfall he wanted to build a snowman. I thought, *how in the world are we going to do that?* But Larry dressed him up warmly and took him out in the snow and put him on the ground and he and Willie built a tiny snowman. It was the cutest thing and Willie was thrilled.

We tried to give him the experiences that most kids take for granted, but it was hard, very hard. We took him swimming and I was holding onto him because he couldn't swim due to his condition and I knew if I let go of him, he'd sink like a rock. He kept saying, "Mom, let go of me," because he just wanted to be like the other kids. Unfortunately, he just couldn't be.

I know all of the things we did to entertain him, to make him feel more like a normal kid, we did both for him and ourselves. When he enjoyed an activity, no matter how small it was, it brightened our hearts perhaps as much as his. It's all part of raising a special needs child.

When it came to caring for Willie, I knew my work would be a life-long commitment. It's a mother's instinct to care for and nurture her young as long as she is here on earth and able to. Afterward, she cares for them from Heaven, watching over them from above.

When my time here on earth is completed, I know I will be able to look the Lord in the eye and say, "Someone will be along after me and he deserves a seat at Your table for he has followed Your will and borne the burdens forced upon him by others, for the sake of others like himself, in Your name."

5

Churchman Chapel—
God's Saving Grace

For where two or three gather in my
name, there am I with them.
—Matthew 18:20

Willie:

Religion and our belief in Our Lord and Savior plays a big role in our family and has no doubt helped us cope with my disability. The Lord seemed to work through the congregation at Churchman Chapel as they have had a terrific impact on our lives. The Church gave me the courage to pursue what others may have considered impossible.

The Church began as a prison ministry outreach through the Evangel Tabernacle and was a non-denominational Church. It sat in the middle of the south-end projects in Louisville, which was a spiritual ground zero because it was surrounded by drug addicts, prostitutes, alcoholics, and many other troubled souls.

In an effort to escape the dregs of their lives they would often come to the Chapel to be saved. In the Lord's own words, "He, who is forgiven much, is loved much." When someone was saved, it was a dramatic event, which I'm sure, urged others to become saved too, while strengthening the faith of those who preceded them in salvation.

The ministry was started by eleven members in a little house on Churchman Avenue. They all must have had an undying love of God and their fellow man to have persevered in such unholy surroundings, but they went to the need like true missionaries do.

I pretty much was raised in the Church. Both Mom and Dad were involved in the music program there. She played the guitar and Dad, the bongo drums. When I was a baby and was taken to Church, and they were busy with their music, it was as if I had been adopted by the entire congregation. You could call me a Church baby. During a service, I would be passed around from one loving pair of arms to another. They couldn't get enough of me, so I never lacked for love. I can't imagine how many kisses I got in those days.

When a new pastor was needed, the Lord, in His way, spoke to the Church Elders that Mike Duke should be the next Pastor, so he was appointed. He was definitely a departure from what one would consider a man of the cloth, given his background as the former president of a motorcycle gang, but he was a plain-spoken man with an abundance of common sense, which drew many to hear him preach.

He was also a humble man - truly a man of God. He was a big influence in my life, and he loved me like I was his own son. Fortunately, Mike and his wife, Kathy, were like another set of parents to me.

From the influence of the members of Churchman Chapel, I learned that people don't have to be pushing you in a direction to make a profound difference in your life. It is often by example. This Church took in the underprivileged, the downtrodden - those who needed a helping hand. Many had obstacles in their lives that were difficult to overcome and that others would have run away from, but they worked tirelessly, silently, and selflessly with the help of God to overcome their demons. What better example for me than to follow their lead and to take God's hand to show me the way.

The love and support shown me at Churchman Chapel enabled me to accept the support of my wrestling team brothers, to know and understand their intentions. At the same time, it showed me that my role on the team could be one of silent example, one who could persevere under exceptional physical and emotional challenges and lead them.

Brenda:

Churchman Chapel is where I found God. I grew up in a Christian home – a typical Baptist one. When I was nineteen, my rebellious side bloomed. I didn't do drugs or alcohol or anything like that, I just resisted control by others. I wanted to do my own thing.

Unfortunately, I went through a lot of relationships with men. When I share my testimony with others, I tell them I was "looking for love in all the wrong places." I didn't write the song, but I surely lived its lyrics.

A lot of my poor choices were the result of my own low self-esteem. Often I thought a man would love to have a woman like me who owned her own home and was making a good living as a nurse. But many of them saw me as a woman who they could use and throw away. I learned the hard way.

An acquaintance of mine, after he found out I had broken up with a long-term boyfriend, called and asked me to come to Churchman Chapel with him. I told him I didn't want anything to do with it, being with what I thought was a bunch of church-going hypocrites, me not being familiar with their ministry.

I was out shopping at a local mall and a woman approached me and said, "Excuse me, the Lord told me to tell you to read Psalm 91." Of course, I looked at her like she was crazy and simply replied, "okay." I was curious what Psalm 91 was, so when I got home, I checked the only Bible I had, a Gideon Society one which I had from years earlier at the hospital where I worked.

I read Psalm 91 which says the Lord is our Protector and decided to go ahead and attend a service at the Chapel. There I heard contemporary Christian music, which I had never heard before. I fell in love with it. Since I play guitar, it was a natural attraction. In the middle of their song service, they announced they were going to sing Psalm 91. I thought to myself, *they're singing my song. This is where I need to be!*

Pastor Duke began preaching how a person should look at another's fruit – to not get involved with someone who has rotten fruit. You want a man or woman with character. I felt like he was talking directly to me. I had experienced, firsthand, rotten fruit people. As a result, I wound up pledging the rest of my life to Christ, and the rest is history. Pastor Duke was such a compelling speaker; it seemed like someone was saved every week when he was preaching God's Word, so he undoubtedly had an impact on the many lives he touched.

After I was saved, I began praying for my ex-boyfriend who was spiritually lost. I went to Pastor Duke and told him that every time I started praying for him to be saved, I would cry, not because we had broken up, but because he was lost – he didn't have Jesus in his life.

He told me that's a prayer burden and when you have prayed enough God will speak to you and tell you, *that's enough*. Sure enough, when I was praying one day, the Lord spoke to me in my mind and said, "That's enough." I followed His word.

Other churches teach their members to simply recite prayers. But we're made in God's image and the second part of true prayer is not only to ask the Holy Spirit into your life but to simply give God a chance to speak to you in whichever way He chooses, and He will.

Some people listen with an intent to respond and aren't paying attention to what He's saying. They miss the point that it's not a debate, it's to follow His will.

Churchman Chapel played a big role in both Willie's and my life. The Lord even brought Larry and me together there as husband and wife. The role Mike and Kathy Duke have played in our lives can't be understated. They and their ministry have been a blessing from God.

6

My Brothers—My Lifeline

How good and pleasant it is when
God's people live together in unity!

—*Psalm 133:1*

Willie:

Despite our practices being hard and tedious, I always enjoyed the camaraderie of my teammates and coaches, both being around and joking with them. They were great guys and while we were a team, we were also like a band of brothers. They were my lifeline.

I couldn't have wrestled if they hadn't taken me under their collective wings and helped raise me up. I owe them more than they know. They motivated me by the way they treated me, all of them – warriors tending to one of their own. I was on the team, so I was one of them. No questions.

But they weren't just teammates and coaches, they were my support group too - always there when I needed help, never complaining, always diligent. They willingly accepted their responsibilities as if it was an unspoken acknowledgment of the conditions they imposed on themselves to be a member of the team.

But more importantly, they considered me their peer, a hard-nosed wrestler. They knew I wouldn't have been there if I didn't deserve to be. I didn't have all the physical tools at my disposal like them, but I was no less their equal in their eyes. Sometimes the only difference between the impossible and the possible are those who support you. I owe a lot to my teammates and coaches for the way they supported and helped me succeed. Brothers to the end!

Our relationship allowed me to be myself, so I was always joking and cutting up. I was comfortable in my role as a team leader and genuinely proud when I was voted a team captain in my senior year. That said it all about the hearts and souls of my teammates and the entire wrestling program for me to have such an honorable distinction.

I think I won the title not only for my motivational ability but also for my wrestling intellect. My teammates knew I knew the technical aspects of wrestling as well as any of them, which many of them thought was pretty amazing.

When I would be sitting on the sidelines while one of them was wrestling, I would shout out moves for them to execute. I could visualize the proper moves for different situations, but in my own matches, I just couldn't execute them because of my disabilities. I was truly a student of the sport. As a result, the team respected, praised, and followed me.

***

I was also constantly playing practical jokes on them and I must admit, I went over the top many times. But they never wasted an opportunity to retaliate, either.

We often wondered what others thought of us when we were at tournaments and other teams and supporters saw my own teammates teasing me or getting physical and swatting or jabbing at me. They were probably thinking, *What are they doing to that poor kid in the wheelchair, beating up on him? The thugs!* They had no idea what was actually transpiring, that they were just getting even with me for the good-natured abuse I was constantly dishing out to them.

Once we were at a tournament and an underclassman was helping me get weighed in and giving me assistance getting into my wrestling singlet. All the while I was giving him grief, barking at him, "Hurry up, you're going too slow," the normal razzing you'd give an underclassman. We were both laughing about it.

A reporter from the *Courier-Journal*, a local Louisville newspaper, came by and asked if my teammates always helped me get dressed. I replied, "Yes, they do, but I always have this one help me because he has Barbie dolls at home which he dresses up, so he is especially good at helping me get dressed."

We saw the reporter write down my response and when he was gone, we both laughed, wondering if he had taken the bait and my quote would show up in the morning paper. It didn't, but it didn't stop me from joking with my teammates and anyone else whenever I could. It was my shtick.

I also used my wheelchair to my advantage, when possible, in my joking and teasing. One time after a hard practice there was a basketball game in progress in the gym. I was waiting for my ride home, so I was hanging out watching the game with one of my teammates. I was thirsty after our hard practice and wanted a cold drink, but I had no money to buy one at the concession stand.

He pulled out a couple of dollars and told me to get a bottle of water and a hamburger or a hotdog or something else to eat. When he went to hand me the money, as I reached for it, he jerked it away. Actually, something I would probably have done to someone else, myself. He was just playing with me. He didn't intend to give me any money. It was, no doubt, a payback for some joke I must have played on him at some time.

Once, when he waved it, I was able to grab it and we were pulling it back and forth between us. Being the master jokester I was, I yelled out for everyone to hear, "Help me, he's trying to steal my money," in as helpless a sounding voice as I could muster, and turned the tables on him.

A big guy walked up and saw me in the wheelchair and said, "Do we have a problem here?" I replied, "Yes, he's trying to steal my money!" My friend tried to plead his case to no avail, so he released his grip on the money and I proceeded to use it to buy a bottle of water and a hot dog. I knew there'd be another payback coming, but it was fun, anyway.

Joking was just part of my makeup. I made the coaches laugh as much as my teammates. They all said I was crazy. Coach Jarvis used to laugh about my personality, which ran between humorous and goofy, depending on the situation.

One time Coach was giving instructions to one of my teammates throughout a match and I was behind him yelling, "Coach! Coach!" trying to get his attention. He kept ignoring me, but I continued trying to get him to turn around.

Finally, when the match was over and he shook the other kid's hand, he turned around to see what I kept nagging him about. I was pointing at the biggest handicap sign I've ever seen, the official one with the blue background and a white silhouette of a stickman in a wheelchair. I was sitting right in front of it yelling, "Coach, it's a portrait of me!" He couldn't help but laugh. He enjoyed my sometimes outrageous humor as did others.

When one of my other coaches, Ken Maupin, would shake my hand, acknowledging me for a job well done, I'd pull my hand away and blurt out, "Ewww"! It was silly, but I did it every time.

In retaliation, he and some others called me Justin Timberlake of Fairdale Wrestling because when I let my hair grow out, I had a look that resembled Timberlake's hairstyle. I was always patting my "fro." If others wanted to help me with things, I'd always pat them on the back of their head. Silly? Sure. Sarcastic? Absolutely. Harmful? No way.

My sense of humor extended past wrestling and was prominent in the rest of my high school life. The teachers at Fairdale High all loved me and my sense of humor, a permanent part of my personality. In my junior year, I was elected one of the princes in the Homecoming Court, so I started signing all my schoolwork papers Prince William, Fresh Prince of Fairdale. They thought it was funny, as did I. In my senior year, I was elected Homecoming King. I enjoyed the promotion!

Another time I was wheeling myself through the gym to the wrestling room during volleyball season. I teased the girl's volleyball coach, Ms. Matos, that volleyball wasn't real a sport, because it's not tough like wrestling is. The next time I came through the gym she, as well as the whole team, playfully bombarded me with volleyballs. I never told her volleyball wasn't a sport, ever again. I got the message. It was funny – I deserved it!

If it comes easy to you, and it does me, a sense of humor is a good skill that can be used to communicate with others. Everyone understands humor and a little well-timed good-natured jab here and there can be just the right touch. It's hard to be unhappy when you're laughing, either with someone or at yourself. I choose happiness and laughter. Even silliness at times has a place in a serious world.

Humor can also be a good diffuser of anxious feelings and emotions. It can help relax others who may be uptight around a disabled person. And it can be very uplifting to those who struggle with disabilities because it helps them cope with their pain and physical problems.

I have no humility or embarrassment about being in a wheelchair. It is my life and humor has a big role in it. It is my secret sauce – the spice of life! I'm going to stick with humor until it doesn't serve me anymore, which I hope is never.

My incessant joking and teasing were also like bonding glue for the team. It sometimes held us together. With humor, I could brighten up each day and find common ground with both my coaches and teammates. If I could be funny with all I was dealing with, why couldn't they lighten up and enjoy our time together?

And there was a notable uniqueness to it since it came from the most unlikely candidate, a handicapped team member you expected to exist in the shadows of its best performers. That made it special to our team which made it more desirable and accepted. I had my favorites to ride, but no one was exempt – I got on everyone. It was good for the team's spirit and for me.

**

Despite all of the pranks we played on each other, wrestling is truly a brotherhood. Brotherhood builds morale, camaraderie, and pride - all critical to a team's success. It was most evident on our team.

There is an unspoken special bond amongst wrestlers, not just those on the same team, but with opponents as well. It is the ultimate *mano a mano* sport. We are like gladiators in the ring, our ultimate goal being the conquest of the other, but doing so in a highly respectful way, within a self-imposed code of honor.

We're just different than other athletes. Dan Gable, the well-known, successful collegiate and Olympic wrestler once said, "Once you've wrestled, everything else in life is easy." It's true. It takes a special type of person to be a wrestler. It's more than just being physically strong or quick because it beats you down if you're not mentally tough enough to meet its challenges.

From the practices in high temperatures every single day to running drills until you dropped, to intense wrestling against your teammates so you'd qualify to wrestle in the next matches. It's a grind, but it prepares you for battle like nothing else could.

They call us grapplers for a reason. We grab, we hold onto our opponents, we struggle for a dominant position with every move. Wrestling is a grungy dirt-in-your-face exercise. It's not fancy – no cheerleaders, no pep bands. It's not like any other sport.

We're also in constant physical contact with our opponent. We feel them, we smell them, and we use the closeness between us to sense their next move. We hear their breathing, grunting, and groaning. And they hear ours. There's little separation between you and them.

At times it seems we can feel their heart pounding like our own, as we both struggle for a superior position against the other. It's nearly animal-like with one purpose, one focus – defeating the other. Each time out is six minutes of the fight of your life.

There is no special equipment. No fancy shoes, no gloves, no belts, just your bare hands, your arms, your legs, your strength, and ability, but most of all your desire, your inner being, your heart, your will to succeed. You're out there on the mat alone, responsible for your own actions and results. It may seem primitive, but that's much of its appeal – it's natural.

Will you prevail or will your opponent? Dan Gable also said that the first period of a match is won by the best technician, the second by the kid in the best shape, and the third by the kid with the biggest heart.

What a rush, what a feeling, just to be competing. If you win, it's heaven. If you lose, you suck it up and give it everything you've got next time. It consumes you physically and mentally. I loved it. It elevated me, gave me purpose, and gave me hope!

But wrestling is also an attitude, a state of mind, an acknowledgment that if you aren't tough enough, you won't succeed. While it's a battle against another, it's also a battle against oneself. Can you survive and succeed? Are you tough enough?

For all others and most athletes, if you break your nose or cut an eye open, you run to clean it up. For a wrestler, it's considered a badge of honor – you feel proud. I loved it when I got cross-faced extra hard and had my nose bloodied. It made me feel tough and motivated me even more.

Wrestling is also fundamentally different from other sports. For example, a basketball player runs, dribbles, shoots, passes to other players and competes in a game. It's highly technical and requires speed, agility and a high degree of hand-eye coordination to be successful.

Taking nothing away from the demands of other sports, wrestling though is a lifestyle. You must change your body to compete. You watch your weight and develop certain muscles to be successful. Your body's chemicals change – you become addicted to it!

Wrestling is not just a seasonal thing, either. You have to be involved in it year-round and make it part of your life if you're going to have any success. Our coaches always said you have to be a little bit crazy to wrestle because of the stress and demands it constantly puts on your body. As they say, "Crazy is as crazy does."

Wrestlers also walk and talk differently. They exude the self-confidence and pride that you would expect to see in any successful warrior. Many in school wanted to wrestle because it sounded exciting. But it's not the same as wrestling with your brothers or friends on your living room floor, so once they got there, they realized what they were up against, and most couldn't handle it.

It's a very small select group who can succeed in the sport. As a result, you express yourself with more confidence, a certain self-assurance that you carry with you even after your wrestling days are over. You never *were* a wrestler, you always *are* a wrestler. It's our lifestyle and we're proud of it.

Wrestlers are also fighters in their own right. We're not throwing punches, but we are going up against each other, one on one. The individual competition also generates a long-lasting bond with your opponent. Some say they remember certain moves made against them or they themselves made, years after a match. I know I do.

After you've wrestled for a number of years and you run into a former opponent, you share a special bond with them as a result of your match, despite having been competitors with only one of you being the victor. It provides special memories and later triggers conversations due to the connection, not only because you competed against the other, but also because wrestlers are a very special select group.

You also have a bond with anyone else who has ever wrestled. Many famous people, including presidents, were wrestlers. Some call wrestling the oldest and greatest sport the world has ever known. It sure is special to me.

One of my best friends from high school and wrestling was Tristan. He was a year younger than me and we both wrestled on the same team. We hung out a lot together and had good times. We were like brothers.

He said things were more serious on the team after I graduated and the team missed having me around. We're still friends but don't talk as much. After he graduated, he went away to school on a wrestling scholarship, so he was pretty consumed with that.

While we were in Fairdale together, we hung out a lot outside of wrestling, too. Once he invited me over to his house to play his NBA 2K video game. He wondered how I was going to play because of my bad hand. I told him I would be okay. He was surprised when I had to hold the controller in an unusual way, but then I started beating him at his own game. He wondered what was going on and had to get serious or get thumped.

He used to carry me up and down stairs depending on what we were doing or where we were going and I'd be laughing and rocking back and forth trying to make him fall. Guys do goofy things together. Over time, he pushed me miles in my wheelchair, up to McDonald's and back, or over to our other friends and back. He was my legs, but it was like I was walking – always on the move. We went everywhere. Wherever he went, I went. It didn't matter, we were good friends.

Tristan hit a few rough patches over time, made some bad choices, but I was there for him as he always was for me. That's what friends do – they're there for each other, just like brothers.

***

I came to understand the meaning of brotherhood and special relationships from my time with the Duke family. Being an only child dealing with a disability that was changing as I was growing up, I needed more care and attention than the average child, both physically and emotionally. It helped me immensely to be with them nearly every day.

Since they had six children and some were near my age, I learned a lot of social skills being around and interacting with them on many levels. Everything they did, I did, whether it was doing crafts or just playing games. I was just one of the family and their older kids took very good care of me, especially Sarah and Emily.

Kathy made me a Batman cape which I wore constantly and they'd run carrying me through their house with my arms outstretched like I was flying. Acting like a superhero with special powers is a good outlet for children who struggle just to walk. It frees them from their disabilities and allows them to dream, if only for a moment, which fuels their hopes for the future – a more normal life.

Mike, himself, took me under his wing and was a major supporter of mine. He encouraged me to do things I never thought I could. It may be where I developed a lot of my determination – his pushing me.

Once when all of the Duke children ran upstairs to play and I got left behind downstairs in my wheelchair, I asked Mike if he would take me upstairs. He replied, "You can get up there yourself. Go on." I stared up the steps wondering how I could possibly climb all the way to the top but I had no choice if I wanted to be with the others, so I gave it a go.

It was like he released me to the challenge. He knew what he was doing. I started crawling and was making steady progress and I looked back to see if he was watching me in case I fell, but he wasn't. I found out later he was but didn't let me see him.

I made it all the way to the top and I was laughing and all excited and proud of myself and turned around and shouted, "Mike, Mike, I made it!" He was as happy for me as I was. I never got left behind when the kids ran upstairs ever again, thanks to him. I learned that trying to keep up is as important as keeping up.

Recalling life-changing moments like this motivated me not only to endure my endless therapies, but also to overcome the rigors of wrestling practice. It showed my brothers on our wrestling team that I had what it took to compete, to stand with them.

It wasn't easy for the Dukes to take me in the way they did. They had their own hard times having six kids, plus me all week, but they did it because they knew it was good for me and felt it was their calling.

Kathy always wanted to help me be as much of a kid as I could, and having six other children, she knew what it entailed. She always had me involved as much as I possibly could be with her other children. She knew my limitations, but she did her best to help me push past them. I made so much improvement in my physical abilities under her watchful eye. I was truly like her seventh child, and she one of my mothers.

The Dukes were the first to teach me the true meaning of brotherhood just by the way they lived - their feelings of love, friendship, and support, which can lift others over many obstacles in their lives. When I got to Fairdale High and joined the wrestling team, I knew what I needed to do to belong in their brotherhood.

***

The bond of brotherhood also extends to your coaches. While you have a special relationship with teammates, each year some come and go but your coaches are with you through all four years and teach you wrestling skills as well as life lessons through their example.

Coaches Liu, Maupin and Boyd were exceptional as was Joe Jarvis. Joe was my coach in both my junior and senior years. He told me coaches Liu and Maupin deserved the most credit for my pursuit of wrestling because they gave me my chance in the beginning. He said they were the ones who saw a kid with a wrestler's heart, not a disabled kid in a wheelchair and opened the door for me to be on the team.

They all knew what I was up against, but each took it on as their own personal challenge. Though they didn't look at me as disabled, they did look after my personal safety. They helped me with exercises when my teammates were doing other drills. Their goal was to do whatever they could to help me succeed, not just on the mat, but in life.

If they hadn't looked after me as they did, I would never have become a wrestler, which was the catalyst for me to overcome the challenges of my disabilities. They were the ones who saw the real me. I owe a lot to them, more than they know.

I found out later that, in my junior year, the coaches discussed what they could possibly do to help me be able to walk, even if with crutches, on my Senior Night. They decided collectively to work very hard on strengthening my legs and bulking up my arms more. That was their goal. Unfortunately, they weren't able to overcome the permanent effects of CP and I wasn't able to walk on Senior Night, but it wasn't for their lack of effort and concern.

I was very fortunate to have these positive role models in my life. They taught me, I am who I am, and downplayed their own roles in my life. But my coaches were all outstanding men and played a big part in my life and development. They admired my determination, my heart and refusal to quit, no matter the odds.

Walk with the wise and become wise,
for a companion of fools suffers harm.

—*Proverbs 13:20*

Brenda:

Willie used to talk to me about his wrestling team and coaches. "They're my brothers," he'd say. It was like they were all on a mission - proud of what they were doing regardless of the results. I didn't come to appreciate what he meant until later when I saw how they looked after him but not in a sympathetic, feel-sorry sort of way, but more as a self-imposed duty - a responsibility to their own. He was one of them, period.

To see how his teammates looked after him and helped him change his clothes and go to the bathroom without anyone telling them to do so, was quite impressive. They weren't a heavenly host of angels by any means, but God bless them that they acted like gentlemen the way they did with him. It sure made it easier than if they would have left him to tend to himself. If so, he may have had to quit the team since he needed so much help.

I was also happy he had a group to identify with. As an only child who wasn't interacting with brothers and sisters daily at the time, and who wasn't as mobile as other kids his age, it filled a void in his life in many ways.

Willie always thought all the time he spent with the Duke kids prepared him for being part of a team. I think it did too. He received an education in social interaction with others.

You can pretty much see who accepts Willie now. Some shy away from him and any resulting duties that may come with being his friend. While others who would be in our home visiting will come to me and say, "Brenda, we put Willie in bed for you." Some who had been out with him would push him in the kitchen through the back door and say, "Brenda, Willie's here. Bye." Then there are other kids you could tell didn't want anything to do with lifting him or anything like that.

We've learned that when you have a disability, you can't force people to accept you or your condition. Some do immediately, but others take more time - it's human nature, I'm sure. There's no sense in reading more into it than there is. At the same time, it's delightful and makes you proud of your fellow man when you experience those who immediately embrace the needs of another – the true meaning of brotherhood.

My team—my brothers.

7

Living with a Disability—
Physical and Emotional Challenges

Trust in the Lord with all your heart and
lean not on your own understanding

—Proverbs 3:5

Willie:

If you think physical disabilities are limited to just that, they aren't. They're hard psychologically and tough on your soul, your inner being. Friends and supporters can go a long way to ease some of the pain. And while the pain may change as we age, it never goes away completely.

If you're disabled and you make a friend, they'll probably be a good one because they've accepted you and your limitations. They're not fickle and will be a long-term friend to be cherished.

Young children can be uncomfortable around someone with a disability, but others see past it and simply see another playmate. I never understood whether it was their upbringing or their individual personalities. Maybe it was both. Either way, if someone wanted to play with me, I was all for it. I didn't need to know why. Kids need other playmates. It's important for their physical and emotional development.

I couldn't have had it any better having the Duke kids for playmates. My favorite buddy was Timmy who was a few years older than me and also had a slight case of CP. I felt very comfortable around the Dukes. When you are young and have a disability, other kids don't know how to accept or interact with you. But with the Dukes, I was just another playmate. It was very helpful for my physical and social development to have them surround me the way they did.

They treated me like all the other kids, but since I was the youngest, I think I was their guinea pig for some adventures. One time they conned me into sliding down the steps from the second floor of their home in a cardboard box. I went sailing down the steps at breakneck speed and when I reached the bottom, I shot across the floor and slammed into the front door.

Mike Duke was sitting in the living room and looked over at the ruckus and shook his head without saying a word. I poked my head out from inside the box and shouted, "That was fun!" They were always doing things like that with me. I loved it!

Since they took me everywhere they went I not only got to experience things I otherwise wouldn't have, but I got to do it with other kids too, which was a big bonus! I was always in a wheelchair even when we were playing, but it didn't matter to them since we grew up together and they were used to it. The wheelchair was also a lot smaller since I was smaller, which was a good thing, so it rarely impeded our escapades.

Once, Timmy and I went to the nearby community center where we could play ball. When we arrived, he began pushing me around in my wheelchair very fast, which was fun until he tried to turn sharply and I flipped over and hit my head on the ground. He panicked and ran away and left me laying there, crying, but a police officer came by and helped me up.

Timmy had run home and told Kathy, so she came running with an ice pack for my head and to see for herself what had happened. I was sitting there with a big goose egg on my head. Timmy had run away because he thought he'd be arrested by the police officer for tipping me over. Kid stuff; fond memories, though.

Other children were uncomfortable around my wheelchair. Perhaps it was a device they just didn't understand. When I would be with the Duke children, who lived near a community center, there were always plenty of kids there to play with. However, I didn't have many friends near where I lived. Many of the kids there were afraid to play with me. Maybe they feared they would hurt me. Who knows?

In elementary school, kids didn't know what to make of the wheelchair – or how to approach me. I sometimes thought they looked at me like I was a mutant. But of course, when you're a kid, you wouldn't know about wheelchairs and walkers and the like unless you have been around them. The kids were curious and would ask me lots of questions. If you can believe it, one even asked me if I was born in a wheelchair! Kids with disabilities just want to have fun and play and have friends like all the other kids do. I know I did. Some are lucky to make friends as I was, probably because of my outgoing personality.

My dad was very protective of me and would become upset if other children would shun me because of my condition, especially if they were in our extended family.

One time we were at a niece's wedding and I wanted to get out of my little wheelchair to go play with the other kids. Dad decided to get me out and walk me over so I could socialize with them. One of my older cousins saw that he had gotten me out of the chair, sat me on the floor and held onto one of my hands to lead me across the floor to them.

He could see that I was excited to be able to go and be with the group, but as we approached, he led the younger kids away and they ran to the other side of the room. My disappointment at what occurred was evident, and Dad was upset by their actions. He was always my protector, but he was angry and probably ashamed by what we had witnessed.

Another time he took me to a car show and put me in a bouncy house and all the other kids got out and left me in it alone. Maybe they saw me as a freak, or maybe they were afraid of bouncing into and hurting me. Either way, I was alone in a bouncy house, where the fun is bouncing around with other kids.

Situations like these can sometimes be harder on the parents than the child. It's difficult for a parent to explain to a child why others don't want to play with them.

But not all kids knew how to relate to me. I was different. If they hadn't encountered a person with a condition like mine before it could be uncomfortable or confusing to them and their first reaction would be to back away because they didn't know how to deal with it - nothing more than that. When you were a kid were you around anyone in a wheelchair? How did you treat them? Did they make you uncomfortable?

Dad always said I was a peacemaker and saw the good in everyone, so he was especially pleased when the Duke children accepted me into their family the way they did. All they saw was me – no wheelchair, no walker, and no braces. I think Dad thought all children should treat me the same way. It's a good thought but not very realistic.

Some of my teachers actually had a certain inborn prejudice about a disabled child in a wheelchair. Mom had trouble getting me into regular classes in my early years. Some considered me severely disabled and sometimes assigned me to classes with mentally disabled children.

Mom fought it and got me into regular classes. The teachers and administrators weren't looking past the wheelchair and my speech impediment. Mine was primarily a mobility issue, not a mental one.

Many often form fixed opinions about those in wheelchairs. Let's face it: the international symbol of a disabled person is a stick figure in a wheelchair. It's ingrained in our brains and the widespread use of the symbol alone can leave a permanent impression in people's minds.

There are many reasons you need a wheelchair since it is primarily a means of transportation to improve mobility. But many seem to think when a child or young person is in a wheelchair, they're also mentally challenged. Again, their opinion may be prejudiced, because some in wheelchairs do have mental issues, but most don't.

I think people, in general, find it difficult to talk to someone with a disability because they don't know what to say and don't want to hurt their feelings. I can tell they're wondering, *what happened to you?* But they're hesitant to ask. I also believe some think disabilities are embarrassing to the affected, so they refrain from inquiring and then form their own opinion about their condition. I'd prefer they ask, rather than wonder or gawk out of curiosity. Have you ever asked a stranger about their disability? No, probably not.

It's normal though, to wonder what causes someone to be in a wheelchair. Have you ever stared at a disabled person, in wonderment, because they were different? Not like from a foreign country, but different in a way you don't know. If you see a grandma or grandpa in a wheelchair, you instantly figure they're frail. If you see a young person in a wheelchair what do you think? It's not normal to see a young person in a wheelchair, period. Therefore, many people don't know how to react to it. And if someone doesn't know how to react to anything in their life, their first reaction probably won't be the best one.

Sometimes, when others talk to me about my disability, they end the conversation with "I'm, sorry." Often I'll reply, "There's no need to apologize – I'm not looking for pity." A helping hand now and then when we need it is nice, but another's pity doesn't lighten our load, in fact, it often increases the burden we feel.

I also regret when others dote on us. We've learned to cope with our limitations. Sometimes I let others help me even when I don't need it, so it makes *them* feel better. Good people like to help others. If they feel better about themselves by helping me, I've done a good deed, so I'm okay with it.

It is interesting that in addition to dealing with our disabilities day in and day out, we also have to deal with the perception of our disabilities by others. What? Don't we have enough to contend with? Do I have to worry about how you feel about me? I genuinely like most people and know they mean well, but it's not always easy being nice. Truth is, I'm happy with who I am and the way I am.

Many of those who don't know me lower their expectations when they're around or interacting with me. Even though they mean well, it can feel insulting and demeaning.

When I was a teenager, others would approach me and speak very slowly, as if I didn't understand what they were saying. They didn't expect me to be normal mentally. They had placed me in a less capable category. Too bad. I've got more to offer than they gave me credit for.

Unfortunately, in addition to my other physical limitations, I have the challenge of a stutter. It surfaces mostly when I try to talk too fast, or have to use certain words, or am getting out of breath from a long sentence, among other triggers. It is perhaps now my biggest challenge to overcome so I can communicate better with others. A long, difficult stutter when speaking with someone who doesn't know me will probably affect their perception of me. I'm aware of this and try to avoid my stutter trigger points, but it remains a challenge for me and always will.

There are drugs to combat some of the symptoms of CP. A friend of mine took Baclofen to help keep his legs from straightening when he speaks, a common symptom. I suffer, as many people with CP do, from the same condition. I wouldn't take the drug because I could see it made him drowsy and I didn't feel it was a good trade-off for the relief from the symptom.

As we age and our circle of acquaintances does too, interaction with others gets easier. When you are in certain situations, in middle or high school, for example, the students know you are required to meet established qualifications to be in their class, so they no longer wonder as much about your mental faculties. They're also older and have experienced others with disabilities and may be more educated about their situations.

Mom would often tell me she wished she could trade places with me. I think some of it was driven by when she would see the longing on my face when I was watching other kids play basketball or other games in which I couldn't participate. I told her often I would never want her to trade places with me because this is the life God gave me, not her. And I wouldn't want her to go through what I have. Although I can live with it, I wouldn't wish it on anyone else.

This is the mountain God gave me to climb, and the strength to climb it, so I would never want to trade places with anyone else. All things considered, I'm happy with my life, but it doesn't mean I don't have my own personal battles to overcome.

***

For those with a disability, therapy often becomes a way of life, a necessary grind, but that's if you're fortunate enough to have the means or access to a good therapy program. I did through the Kosair Cerebral Palsy Kids Center, a wonderful institution. I believe firmly as do others that the grind of continuous therapy, week in week out, made me as tough mentally as it did physically. I'm sure it got me ready for the rigors of wrestling. You have to want it for its own sake.

Long-term therapy doesn't give you the instant gratification that rehabilitation therapy can and no miracle is likely to occur as a result. You aren't going to return to your former good health. You're trying to offset or minimize a debilitating condition and without it, you may regress into a worse state. It's a game of inches and it's definitely not a sprint – it's a marathon. Have you ever had to undergo physical therapy to recover from surgery or an injury? Can you imagine going through therapy from birth, not knowing when, if ever, it would end? It's a tough row to hoe, for sure.

My first three years of medical bills were paid for by First Steps, which was a godsend. It's a Kentucky early intervention system that provides services to children with developmental disabilities from birth to age three, as well as their families. Early intervention is invaluable.

I received the best care at Kosair for my physical, visual, and speech therapy. Ms. Jamie Ramsay, my physical therapist, was wonderful. She treated me from age one until I started high school and I owe a lot to her and her treatments, both physically and emotionally. When a patient experiences progress with their physical abilities, it helps them tremendously emotionally and provides them with the motivation to continue with their often grueling physical therapy.

My normal routine for many years was to rise in the morning, go to therapy, go to school, and then return after school for more therapy. Then I had to go home and do therapy homework until almost 10:00 at night because every therapist gave assignments for the parents to do with their children.

It was a big commitment for everyone involved, but it paid big dividends and I can't imagine where I'd be today without it. At the same time when I look back on my childhood, that's what I remember most, going to therapy. I feel the time I spent in therapy in some ways took away from my childhood, but I had no choice but to do it – for my own good.

All things considered, I had a pretty normal childhood, but other kids didn't have to endure multiple therapy sessions each week and then continue the therapy drills at home as I did. They had time just to be a kid and do kid things - play with friends, watch cartoons, or otherwise take it easy.

There were times when I was young I wondered why other kids didn't have to go through what I did. Young minds sometimes have difficulty understanding or accepting their plight, and are constantly trying to reconcile circumstances in their lives that they don't feel are fair. I not only had to endure therapy, but I had to be serious about it. That's not a normal thing for a youngster to have to do over such a long haul, but I did it and I'm proud I did.

I did have good times, too. And I wouldn't have been able to do or enjoy many of the things I did from my childhood or afterward if it hadn't been for Ms. Ramsay and the tremendous care I received from her at the Kosair Center.

The main emphasis in my sessions was trying to improve the coordination, strength, and mobility in my legs, my greatest need. It was definitely an uphill battle, given my condition, but we kept at it week after week, month after month, year after year.

For decades, previous to when I began treatment, therapy was prescribed for one day a week, but after some research into its effectiveness, some therapists looked at it differently and determined it may be better to perform it in intensive bursts. So I was my therapist's experiment for a time – a special project!

She decided I was the perfect candidate since I exhibited a great spirit of hard work and determination, not being a complainer. At one point, I was doing two-hour increments several times a week. For those who have never had physical therapy for any condition, two-hour increments are extremely taxing and require a high level of motivation and stamina.

When I look back at my physical therapy days, I'm proud of what I accomplished because I gave it my all and stuck with it year after year, but it's hard to forget some of the exercises and stretching that I dreaded.

One was when the therapist would stretch out my legs because my hamstring muscles were as tight as guitar strings. With me lying on my back they would straighten and pull my leg straight up. It hurt a lot as I could feel my hamstrings fighting against the pull as my leg went higher and higher.

Once my leg was in the highest position, they would hold it there for ten seconds or sometimes longer - which were the longest seconds of my life. Then they'd do the same on my other leg. Every therapy session began this way. Ugh! I couldn't wait to get to the other exercises, but stretching always came first.

I also participated in summer fitness intensive programs where I would be in a group setting with other kids where we would rotate through different exercises. Stations were set up, manned by college-age volunteers with the therapists, and we would go from one to the other doing leg exercises to back exercises.

Ms. Ramsay said she was always able to make it a fun challenge for me, whereas some children they work with for a long time, tire and complain and whine. That was never the case with me. I never complained. She would joke with me often about how difficult an exercise was. She knew it was hard, but it needed to be. I never once complained about her asking too much of me. I'm sure she asked for more because I didn't complain and I took it on as another challenge. I had to beat it, not let it beat me!

She was also pleased with the way I continually demonstrated my positive attitude to the other patients there for therapy. Since I was a patient for such a long time, I was a role model for many of the other kids. I would often challenge them in relay races to encourage them, to help them with their attitude.

I see most things in life in a positive way. You can tell someone to be positive, but it's much more effective if you show them how. You can find fun in most things in life if you look hard enough, and a positive attitude can carry a person a long way.

I was always serious about everything I did but in a fun way. I wanted to achieve and I worked very hard at it. Experiencing positive results is the best attitude adjustment tool there is. Give yourself a reason to be happy. Make a goal – meet the goal.

Ms. Ramsay and I developed a special relationship over the years since she treated me from when I was a baby to when I was in high school. She took a special interest in me as if I was one of her own children. I loved her for it. It definitely lightened my load.

We felt we had a good time when we worked together. She has said I was the cutest little kid with my curly hair and sweet spirit. I always looked forward to seeing her. She still grabs me by my hair whenever I go by to see her, which I occasionally do for a wheelchair assessment or equipment needs. She was like a third mom to me!

She's told me she'd be happy to sit down with me and help me make fitness be a part of my life. Fitness can be a challenge for the disabled. It's great to have a knowledgeable resource like her. I've had lots of good people in my life to keep me on track! I've been blessed.

Therapy goals are also different when you're young than when you're older. For youngsters, it's about working on mobility, developing more independence for getting in and out of chairs or walkers. As we age, the emphasis is more on incorporating strength and endurance into our routines.

I was fortunate to have a friend, Drew, another CP patient who was in therapy at Kosair with me. He was a couple of years older and was as independent as me. He challenged me at using my walker and other things and we were very competitive with each other. We were pretty much equal in our abilities and I think our competitions fueled my competitive attitude which proved to suit me well. I attempted more and probably accomplished more as a result.

One of my favorite therapies, when I was young, was horse therapy. Who would have thought it? Ms. Ramsay arranged it. Equine-assisted therapy is gaining in popularity. It's different than recreational horseback riding because the horse controls the rider rather than the opposite. It is believed that when the horse walks, the motion constantly causes the rider to adjust to it which promotes strength, balance, coordination, flexibility, posture, and mobility.

I was apprehensive at first, being a little guy on a big horse with my legs barely spanning the saddle, but I adjusted quickly. My favorite horse, of course, was one named Willie, like me. I wanted to have him run, (what was I thinking?) so the instructors let him bop along at a quicker pace for a half-minute or so, with me hanging on for dear life.

That was enough for me! It was the one and only time I asked for a run. The horse therapy, though, was a great break from the monotony and grind of regular therapy, and I loved it. Yee-haw! Giddy up!

***

Many of those with physical disabilities often undergo surgeries to help combat the debilitating effects of their conditions. I was no exception. Any type of surgery is often performed and yields the best results when it's performed on children. If a doctor is able to make a physical correction on a patient at an early age, it has a much better chance of yielding positive results as the body adapts to the change naturally as they grow and age.

I was three years old when I had my first surgery. It's called a selective dorsal rhizotomy. The doctors went in and electrically stimulated certain sensory nerve fibers in my back to locate the muscles they controlled. They then clipped some of them to reverse the spasticity caused by the CP in my right hand which was always balled into a fist, and therefore unusable. As a result, I went from not being able to use it, to gaining 60-70% usefulness.

I'd call the procedure a physical success but being in a hospital undergoing surgery as a three-year-old was quite traumatic. I also have what I call battle scars on my back from the procedure. I made it through it though, and am grateful for the results.

My more difficult surgeries were on my hips which were done when I was three years old. X-rays of my back for the rhizotomy surgery revealed that my hips were displaced from their sockets, another result of the CP. I needed surgery on both hips to have them placed in their sockets and then compression pins inserted to hold them in place. It was a painful process especially for a toddler who didn't understand what was going on or why, but necessary none the less.

When I woke from the surgery, I asked Mom if I could walk. She sadly replied no, not yet, but they were doing all they could for me. Unfortunately, the first pins inserted proved to be undersized and didn't hold, so when I was five years old I had to undergo the entire painful procedure again.

With the surgeries, I learned to endure pain and suffering and disappointment, all attributes that I would need later in my life. While the operations and resulting rehabs were difficult, Ms. Ramsay was by my side through them all and helped me push through the pain and therapy. I know I couldn't have done it without her. She had a very positive impact on me in my recoveries and helped me make significant progress afterward.

**

The most significant effect CP had on me was by far on my legs. They contain the strongest muscles in the body and when their use is diminished or restricted it has a far-reaching impact on most activities a person can perform.

The ability to stand, to walk, and be mobile, plays a major role in our existence and is difficult to live without. Given the legs' role to support a person's weight while moving them forward or backward underscores the demands placed on them. The inability to walk normally or unassisted is the most visible effect of my CP.

I spent most of my young life in leg braces, hoping they would allow me to be able to walk unaided, but they didn't. While some can't run or jump as far or as high as others, most people have the ability to stand and walk without assistance. It's when you lose or never had the ability that your life changes forever and you learn to walk unassisted every day of your life.

I've never given up on my desire or goal to someday walk without assistance. It would mean so much to me that while it may be unrealistic barring a miracle, I refuse to let go of the dream.

When I was four or five years old I would ask my mom, "What's it like to walk?" She told me it's hard to explain. I've used various types of walkers in my life, one when I was younger where I stood but was suspended and now a type where I use my upper body to hold me upright while I use my legs to move forward. I've never been able to walk without the use of walkers.

People often ask me what it's like being disabled. I tell them this has always been my life, so I don't have a personal comparison, only what I've observed of other's lives. I believe it would be more difficult to cope with if I had been able to walk until I was a teenager, and then had been in an automobile accident or suffered some other type of serious injury and lost the ability to walk, and became wheelchair bound. In fact, after all my surgeries and years of therapy, I'm better off now than I was when I was younger.

My Grandpa Puckett on my mother's side played a huge role in my physical development as a child. He picked me up when I got off the school bus at three o'clock in the afternoon and stayed with me until Mom got home from work, from grade school all the way until high school.

He'd always ask me, "Are you ready to get your legs moving?" He was fixated on improving my leg strength in order to give me a chance to walk unassisted. It was so important to him. He worked with me every day.

I would walk with him with my walker down our driveway and down the street to his home where he would have me do push-ups and stomach crunches. He also bought a treadmill for his home that he used to have me walk on.

After I had my back surgery, in order to promote healing, he bought a Jacuzzi and he would get in too, to work with me. He also regularly took me to physical therapy. He wanted me to get better so badly.

I really enjoyed being around him. He was in the Army in World War II and landed in Hiroshima not long after the atomic bomb was dropped. He was a great storyteller and once told a story at a Thanksgiving dinner table about buying a wagonload of apples for the orphans nearby.

He once had a dream in which he saw me walk. He said the two of us were walking down a road and I was all excited and skipping around him and just enjoying myself as we walked.

He said the dream frightened him because everything around him was so indescribably beautiful. When he woke up, he realized the Lord was telling him he would not see me walk here on earth. Maybe his dream was a premonition of seeing me walk in heaven, but not until then.

When I was a little boy, my occupational therapist had me draw a picture. Afterward, she asked me what I had drawn. I told her it was my grandpa fixing me pancakes and bacon. He was always looking out for Mom and me. His influence on me will stay with me for the rest of my life. He was the best grandfather and a great role model.

***

I believe I have the strength or could build up the strength in my legs to walk, but it's my lack of balance and coordination that holds me back more than anything else.

I go to the gym to work on my strength, but I believe Jesus has to be the one to help me be able to walk. It won't happen without His help. I think He's keeping me in my wheelchair because I'm an inspiration to those like me. He's waiting until I accomplish some other things because He knows I'm helping others like myself.

If someone had told me years ago that I'd still be in a wheelchair, I wouldn't have believed them because I would have bet that my will and determination would have allowed me to escape it. However, at the same time, I wouldn't have believed I would accomplish many of the other things I have, either.

From a healthcare professional's viewpoint, it would take a miracle for me to walk unassisted. They don't always discount that miracles can happen, but they go about their business of healing and using therapy to maximize what they have to work with. God does give us answers, but sometimes in ways difficult for us to understand or accept.

I have walked with walkers, but not unassisted. One of my proudest moments was when I was seven years old and aided by my walker and my parent's assistance, I slowly and proudly, for the first time ever, walked into Church. Being able to stand tall and proud is a gift from God, Himself. I cherish each and every opportunity.

When it comes to physical matters like walking, as kids get older, puberty is not their friend. They hit growth spurts not only in height but in size, which can itself be debilitating to them. Gravity then may have been what slowed my chances of walking unassisted. It takes more strength and stamina to do any activity on my feet and when you add three or four inches in height and three or four more inches later and the weight that goes with it, it's like it's sucking you down to the ground.

So now, I could probably get in my walker and make my way around in our house or maybe venture out into the yard, but I could never keep up with my friends if we went out somewhere. So to be functional, I need my wheelchair.

I should probably be realistic and resign myself to the fact that walking with a walker may be the highest level of walking I will ever achieve. It doesn't stop me though from working toward or hoping for a miracle someday.

The rigors of therapy and surgeries and the resulting rehab can be a lonely trek up a seemingly unending mountain. You're forced to go it alone – others can't do it for you. But you can't endure the long hours without the care, concern, and encouragement of those around you, your support group. Their role in your struggle and survival is invaluable.

I believe these challenges, beginning at such a young age, are what toughened me up for wrestling, in fact, I'm sure of it. Not just the physical aspects, but the emotional side knowing my teammates were not only pulling for me but were also celebrating my efforts to succeed. I think it elevated them as much as it did me. I wouldn't be where I am today without my many support groups.

Brenda:

When Willie was very young, I always feared kids were going to make fun of him. There was an incident when the Duke girls were taking him on a walk in his stroller and a couple of teenage boys started making fun of him. It upset the girls, but fortunately, Willie was too young to realize what was going on.

Most kids didn't make fun of him and I'm very thankful for that. It's hard enough dealing with a disability but being made to feel self-conscious about it makes it worse. We've had kids stare at him when he was in his wheelchair wondering what was wrong with him, but not much more than that.

I've had adults come right out and ask me what was wrong with him, but Willie is blessed with a great personality and a sense of humor which may have defused a lot of potential teasers because he is so extroverted and not self-conscious about his condition.

Something that bothered him is when people would deliberately avoid interacting with him because of his disability. He describes it as them making him feel like he is part of the wall and invisible. He's outgoing and likes to interact with people so he may avoid being treated like other disabled people because of his personality.

Willie's surgeries were very hard for us to deal with. It's difficult enough for a three-year-old to cope with never having experienced anything like that. When we were investigating having the rhizotomy surgery I had to argue with a doctor about whether it was even the right thing to do.

From my experience as an ortho-neuro nurse, I had seen its benefits and felt it was best for him to have the back surgery in order to be able to open his right hand. The doctor disagreed so I got a second opinion from a neurosurgeon who evaluated Willie and said he should have the surgery. He said if Willie didn't have the surgery, he would develop additional permanent muscle injury (contractures) as he got older.

The two doctors debated it back and forth but the second doctor won him over and Willie had the surgery. It resulted in his gaining about 60% use of his hand from having no use of it at all. Sometimes you just have to fight for your child.

A side benefit of Willie's rhizotomy surgery on his back when he was only three years old followed by the two surgeries on each hip to have them pinned into their sockets was that it got Larry and I thinking about additional ways to help him.

When Willie was five years old, Larry was searching the internet looking for things that would aid his recovery and benefit him going forward. He came across a device called the Hart Walker. A video which showed children using the walker got him excited that it may be of terrific benefit to Willie to develop his legs and be more mobile at the same time.

It was a device in which the child stood but was suspended which would allow them to use their legs to move themselves and walk, without having to support all of their weight. I thought it would help Willie a lot so I called WAVE 3, a local Louisville TV station and asked a reporter if she had any interest in doing a story on the walker because I thought it would help many other disabled children too who may not have known it existed.

She and I talked about the walker at length and she became very interested in Willie's story, although I had called her about the walker, not him. She said she would consider doing a story on the walker, but was more interested in doing a story on Willie. I was very surprised but agreed.

An entire crew came and was with us for a week. They even sent us with a camcorder when we went to Florida so we could film Willie being measured for the walker.

After a week of being followed by them though, they called on the eighth day and asked if they could come back out. I told them enough was enough. By nature, we're private people. We were tired and didn't know how much longer it would go on. We were grateful for their attention, though, and the newscaster did a great job with the story. The station also kept the parts in about our faith, which pleased us. Their story was complete and did not lack for anything.

Our goal was to get the Hart Walker story told and we succeeded. They came back a couple of times to follow up and have always shown interest in him.

This was the first media interest in Willie's story we experienced but there was much more after he got into wrestling from both the print and news media.

When it comes to Willie walking unassisted, it is the thing people hoped and wished for more than anything else, including ourselves. When Willie had his first hip surgery the first thing he asked me when he woke up was whether he could walk. I told him we'd have to wait and see.

Many have had dreams about Willie being able to walk, including me, his Grandpa and others. I got tears in my eyes when my dad, Willie's grandpa, relayed his story about his dream of Willie walking because I had been praying for a long time that he'd see Willie walk before he passed away because it meant so much to him. Now he'll have to see him walk in Heaven.

In my dream, I was standing at our stove cooking and Willie walked in all excited and yakking about something and stood next to me. It then occurred to me, *he's walking, he's walking!* In the meantime, he wasn't reacting to the fact that he was walking, which surprised me, as he was still carrying on about whatever it was he was talking about. Then I woke up.

When the Lord gives you a dream, you can tell it's from Him. You wake up and think, *Wow, that was the Lord.* You can't always easily interpret its meaning, but you feel His message.

After my own dream, there was a period of time when it seemed like nearly every member of the congregation in our Church approached me to say they also had a dream in which they saw Willie walk. I looked at it as if God was sending me a message through them.

If the Lord sees His way of making it happen, many, including me will be grateful. I never thought it would be so long that Willie's couldn't walk unassisted. I thought, maybe hoped, God was going to heal him sooner.

It was definitely a challenge for Willie and us with all the years of his therapy. No doubt the therapy was necessary and important, but I sometimes felt the therapists thought they had to teach Willie as much as possible while he was young so we could still physically handle him.

At the same time, they knew the government would quit paying for his therapy when he reached eighteen years old, so they had a mission to get in as many sessions as possible for his benefit. As a result, we ended up with physical therapy three days a week, and occupational as well as speech therapy, two days a week.

Later a vision therapist diagnosed Willie with a problem with his eyes. She was proud she had diagnosed his condition as I sat in her office sobbing because it meant more therapy sessions. I know he needed the therapy and we would do it, but it was a real burden getting him to all the sessions for so many years.

Without a doubt, Willie's therapy sessions toughened him up. It's no wonder he gravitated toward wrestling, such a physical sport. He wanted to be part of a group and he wasn't afraid of the physical challenges that went with it because of those grueling physical therapy sessions he endured for so long. I have no idea what made him think he could wrestle since he couldn't stand, but he had the courage to try it.

When I think about the therapy sessions, they went on for more than a decade - day after day, week after week, year after year. You have to accept the small improvements as you go. There are no guarantees on the final results. And the goal of the therapies is to be able to do the things that everyone else does without thinking – walking, talking, getting dressed, all the activities of a normal life.

All the necessary therapies point out how debilitating CP is. It takes away so much from the afflicted, but the therapy gives back so little by comparison. Yet Willie stayed with it, hoping, wishing, and praying that someday he'd be able to walk unassisted.

Horse therapy.

Kosair therapy with Jamie Ramsay on left.

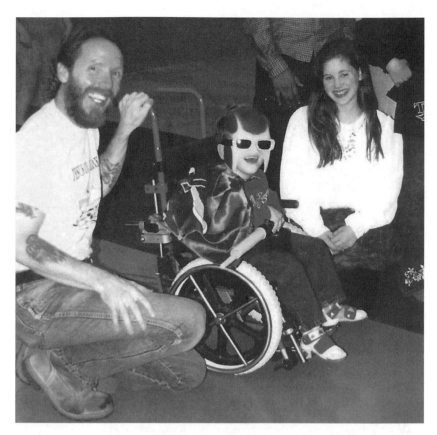

Willie the super hero!

Willie Burton on Hart Walker.

Larry, Brenda & Willie.

8

Motivation for All

Do nothing out of selfish ambition or vain conceit.
Rather, in humility value others above yourselves.
—Philippians 2:3

Willie:

The kind and caring treatment I received from my teammates from the beginning surprised me. As you would expect, these were young, highly competitive testosterone-fueled athletes with one thing in mind, to succeed - not cuddly, caring, choir boy types. But they helped make it possible for me to be on the team.

It was admirable how they accepted me during practices and around the locker room, but it's even more amazing when you're wrestling as a team and the points you win or lose factor into the entire team's overall success. Nevertheless, they treated me as if I was one of their own. I was grateful, but I didn't let it affect my relationships with them.

With me they knew it wasn't all about winning and losing, it was mostly about being on the team – showing effort, giving effort. Coach Maupin once said if they could have an entire team with kids with heart, they'd take it. He said they could teach them the skills needed to win matches. It might take some of them longer than others, but if you have someone with the kind of determination I had, that's how you could build a great team.

My teammates came to respect me for my attitude and what I was going through just to be on the team. I'm sure many of them thought at times, *how does he do it?* I was always at practice, greeting them with a smile and words of encouragement. By the end of many practices, I'd often be the one with the reddest knees, sometimes with cuts. I'd shake it off and tell everyone not to worry about me.

I think they thought I was crazy. I knew I was probably making them endure more than they normally would – making *them* tougher. We all played a role in our team's success; some of us just did it in our own way.

Maybe the biggest example of my persistence is a team practice where I rubbed blisters on my hands. Our team was running laps on the track as usual because it's very important to have strong legs for wrestling. I normally used my walker to do the laps. One day, I forgot to bring it to school with me, so I had to use my wheelchair. It caused me to be late for practice, so when I arrived, Coach Jarvis, one of my coaches at the time, was yelling to me to get started because everyone else was already out running.

He wanted me to get in three laps before the rest of the team had finished. I kept pushing myself as hard as I could to get in the full two miles like everyone else because I didn't want to look like a slacker. I didn't have my gloves with me (actually, I didn't realize they were in my backpack on the back of my wheelchair), so I was developing painful blisters on my hands with each push of the wheels.

After each lap, Coach checked on how I was doing and each time I replied, "I'm fine." He urged me to pick up my pace so I would cover more distance, but he had no idea my hands were hurting as badly as they were. When the rest of the team finished running and I was still on the track, he told them to go out and bring me in, not push my chair, but to jog alongside me to challenge me for the remainder of my lap.

When I finally arrived, Coach saw me looking at my hands which were now raw with bloody blisters and questioned why I hadn't said anything to him before about them. I wasn't about to quit before my teammates were finished running. If I quit because things got tough, they could quit, too. No one could complain about hurting if I was in a wheelchair rubbing blisters on my hands and didn't stop.

Coach nodded as if he understood. I didn't expect my teammates to quit on me and I wasn't going to quit on them. I wanted to show them I could be a leader, too. They got the message. It was worth a few blisters to show them who I was. Blisters heal. Examples live on.

Coach Jarvis and I enjoy a special relationship. He was driving me home from practice one night and I struck up a conversation with his eight-year-old son, who was going to start wrestling the following year.

I was telling him about my biological mother and her issues, my obstacles, my surgeries - my story. I was sitting in the back seat and coach looked back at me in disbelief, like he couldn't believe what he was hearing. I told him, "I'm fine, coach. I'm here and I'm doing the best I can. I'm living, I'm doing great," as I'm relaying my story. He said he couldn't believe I was sitting there with a big smile on my face, that I wasn't fazed by what others would consider an unfortunate life.

They got me out of the car and into my wheelchair, and then into my home. As they were driving home, his eight-year-old son said, "Dad, I don't know how Willie does it. We've talked to him lots of times and you wouldn't know anything bad had ever happened to him. He doesn't act like anything is wrong with him. He just looked like a normal kid in the back seat who we were driving home. I don't know how he stays so positive."

Coach said it's the most vivid memory he has of me because for the first time he learned everything that happened to me to that point in my life. He now knew my story. I think it galvanized our relationship.

***

Since I continued to lose match after match, I feared they thought I was pulling the team down, but to their credit, they never said or gave any indication they felt that way – that I was letting them down. None of them ever acted, "Well, here comes another loss." Rather, they constantly offered me encouragement, no matter my results. They wanted to see me win as badly as I did, but for me, not them.

It was inspiring to be embraced this way. Sports are so competitive by nature, and someone who isn't producing wins, no matter how hard they try, can feel like a failure and a burden to the team.

When I took the mat for each match I always felt in my heart, I could and would win. You'll never win unless you think you can, and you'll always lose if you think you will. I believe my teammates sensed my positive attitude and it may have motivated them in their own matches.

It had to be hard to watch me struggle so badly because at times I got pinned and lost in as little as eight seconds while other times my match would go longer, maybe three or four minutes, raising hopes that were later dashed when I lost. But I never showed that losing fazed me. Simply put, I lost because I lost. It happens.

One of the things I liked about Coach Jarvis was the pep talks he gave before tournaments. He was a good motivator, always trying to bring out the best in us.

He continually reminded me that I didn't have a disability, I had different abilities, and to see that in a positive way, not a negative one. I had special skills so I needed to learn how to use them to my advantage.

It took me a while to believe him, but once I did, it gave me the incentive to use them to my benefit. I knew I was unique and needed to prevail in wrestling my way. I shouldn't focus on the attributes I didn't have, or what I couldn't do, but rather that I had something no one else did.

He was always trying to keep me in a positive frame of mind, not only to perform better but to better accept my losses when they occurred.

I also never looked at myself as disabled, using it as an excuse, and always held my head high before and after each match, despite my continual losses. I think my teammates were often dying inside for me, but they always reassured me, telling me I'd get my opponent the next time out.

With each match I could tell by their enthusiasm and interest, some of them thought I could actually win that week, too. They would take it upon themselves to size up my opponents and give me advice on them and my chances of winning. They'd state, "You can handle this guy, he's scrawny," or, "That guy is slow. Willie, you can win this one." They offered me endless encouragement, and it was sincere and motivated me more than they realized at the time.

***

When I first joined the team, all I wanted was to hang on and stay on the team. I had bigger obstacles to overcome than most of course, but it meant too much to me to fail. So as surprising as it was, I relished the role of a leader – a motivator.

By its nature, it gave me responsibility and filled a need for the team and me. It made me feel like I had a crucial role, not just as a rah-rah cheerleader, but as a contributor to the team effort. It made me feel complete.

As a captain, I was very conscious of my actions, how I acted with the team both on and off the mat. My role was complicated since I didn't have the wins to back it up, but I maximized on effort and kept the others on the team upbeat, which wasn't easy since they were enjoying more success than me.

At times I feared if I continued to lose matches, it would jeopardize the effectiveness of my role. But while I continued to struggle, my teammates continued to stand behind me and I believe it increased my effectiveness, an unexpected benefit.

When we got into the home stretch each season, when everyone was worn out with some even wishing the season would end, I would kick into high gear to keep everyone focused. My motivational technique seemed a bit convoluted for a number of reasons. First, since I was always goofing around, I led the team in practical jokes. But there's a fine line between being humorous and an all-out goof-ball. I had to be conscious of the balance between the two.

Second, I had to rely on my teammates for so much physical assistance. They helped me get dressed, get weighed, carried me on and off the bus and even helped me in the bathroom. While some would consider these duties to be a burden, to them it was motivational. They assumed the responsibilities on their own, without the coaches directing them to do so. They did so with pride, which again speaks to their character.

I was different, as were my needs, and I held a unique role on the team – a leader who required physical assistance. It was definitely an unusual situation for a high school wrestling team, but they did it with pride and a caring attitude.

Just as surprising, most of my teammates looked at me as their *go-to* guy. Whenever they needed a smile or a laugh, they looked to me to brighten their day, and I enjoyed my role. I enjoy being upbeat naturally and brightening other's lives.

Some said it was motivating just to be around me and I made it hard for them to be down. They would be worried about making weight amongst other things, doubting whether they could, and they saw me doing the best I could, and getting beat week in and week out.

They didn't have any excuses for not putting forth an effort with me around, and I wouldn't let them, either mentally or physically. So I'd tell them, straight up.

Everyone likes to slack off a bit now and then, but if they did, they'd see me crawling up and down the mat, and they'd kick it in gear. It's hard to slack off when you see how someone else is handling adversity in everything they do. It motivates others, and I took it on as part of my responsibilities. I could do it better than anyone else because my disability was constantly on display. It wasn't easy, but I did it as best I could. My situation was unique, and I used it to help both the team and me.

***

Don't think that working as hard as I did and losing match after match for years never got me down. I wouldn't be human if it didn't. We all need positive reinforcement in our lives and maybe more if you are faced with, what at times may seem like insurmountable odds. Can you imagine what it was like for me to lose every time I faced an opponent? It wasn't fun.

It had to be difficult for my coaches too, to see me lose as much as I did, and the way I did, especially as hard as they worked with me. I told both Coach Jarvis and Coach Boyd in my junior year that I didn't want my disability to define my character. They understood what I meant and I believe they used it for their own motivation when working with me. It was bigger than just winning or losing. We had another goal!

Coach Jarvis and I had an unspoken agreement between us. He was never going to treat me like I was disabled and I wasn't going to act like I was. We both knew that once either of us did so, it would turn me into a cripple and I would be lost. He was going to treat me like any other kid in the wrestling room, and in return, he expected me to act like everyone else. As a result, I think some of the other kids thought he was too hard on me. If he made them run laps because they weren't performing, he made me do laps in my walker if I wasn't performing either.

One time I came to practice with my walker rather than in my wheelchair. At the time, Coach didn't know I had a walker, or that I could even walk with one. He asked me about it and why I wasn't using it all the time.

I told him sometimes I use it and sometimes I use my wheelchair. He told me I was going to use the walker from that point on and I had better have it with me every day. No more sitting in a wheelchair rolling around the track, I was going to be doing laps with my walker.

In the beginning, I couldn't make one lap around the track. After a while though, I was able to do an entire lap around and then he challenged me to go a mile and I got up to two laps. Sure, he was tough, but he was right. I think my teammates later came to respect how he handled me.

There were times when he had us running circuits in the halls at school. The team would run on the third floor and they took me down on the elevator to the second floor to do the laps in my walker or wheelchair so I wouldn't be in the way or get knocked down by the thundering herd.

Coach would take the rest of the team back to the wrestling room and then realize they had left me on the second floor and have to go back and get me. I was given no special treatment or consideration. I kept doing laps until I was told to quit and they had forgotten me a lot.

Our understanding about his treatment of me was pushed to the limit a few times, though. We would be wrestling with each other and he didn't take it easy on me at all. Other times he didn't think I was giving enough effort and he would push me off my base, knocking me over, yelling, "Get back up, back up, back up." In one of the hard sessions, he accidentally gave me a cross-face hit and bloodied my nose, which we laughed about before we cleaned me up.

The next day, though, I got him back by waiting until he was finished wrestling another teammate. He was sitting and I came up from behind and grabbed him. As a reflex action he dove down toward the floor and I accidentally cross-faced him with my bony right hand and caught him square on his nose. He bled profusely for probably five minutes. He said, "Okay Willie, point made."

That's just how we acted with each other. He allowed me to be myself, and then some – a lot of latitude. Our unspoken agreement that he wasn't going to treat me any differently than any of my teammates, and I wasn't going to act any differently than my teammates, was in full force. If he wrestled another teammate a certain way, he did the same with me. I wasn't given any special treatment because of my condition. I respected him for it and he respected me for not giving up.

***

My teammates were super supportive and were always encouraging me to go deeper and deeper into my matches. They cheered for me like I was the best wrestler in the state. They told me there were times they sensed I might break from the frustration, but they were determined to never let me get to that point. They put forth a concentrated effort to raise my spirits, as I often did theirs.

They were never disappointed with me, but they all agonized with me about my losses. We all knew going in, with my physical challenges, I would have more than my fair share of losses, but we all knew I'd eventually win, or at least we thought I would. We had to keep the faith.

Despite my teammates looking upon me as a motivator, in my junior year, I had gotten down in the dumps and was frustrated about not winning. Although I never missed any practices, I wasn't practicing well and seemed just to be going through the motions. In fact, in my four years of wrestling, I believe I only missed three practices.

One time that season I had a mild cold, not a bad one, so I went to school. I could have gone to practice but didn't. At the end of the next practice, Coach Liu approached me and asked to speak with me for a minute and asked why I skipped practice the previous day. I was honest and told him the cold wasn't a big deal, but I just didn't feel like coming to practice.

He looked me straight in the eye to get my full attention and told me I had to come to practice because he was there because of me. He gave up his time with his family every day to coach us after he got off work and my working through and enduring my challenges made him want to give it everything he had to coach our team.

I was shocked when he said I was the reason he was there every day and if I quit coming, he was going to quit coming, too. It opened my eyes to the commitment we all made to not only ourselves but to the others – the true definition of teamwork.

But still, losing can grind on even the most upbeat individuals, and I was no exception. I don't want to imply I ran the team, but they constantly looked to me for inspiration and motivation and my mood rubbed off on them. In many ways, I was the spirit of the team. If I was down, they were down. If I was upbeat and ready to go, they were upbeat and ready to go.

One time the rest of the team put their heads together to see what they could do to raise my spirits. My mental well-being was very important to them because how the team reacted in practice and matches seemed dependent upon my mood.

My coaches picked up on my then, down mood and seized the opportunity to buoy my spirits, as well as possibly get even with me for many of the practical jokes I had played on the team over time.

One week they began circulating a false rumor that I was going to get cut from the team for not producing, and they were going to tell me Friday. In reality, Coach Boyd had arranged a Skype session for me with Anthony Robles. Anthony is a one-legged wrestler who wrestled in college for Arizona State. For unknown reasons, when he was born to his sixteen-year-old mother, he was missing his entire right leg, all the way to the hip. He had no stump to attach a prosthetic limb to, so he wrestled on one leg.

He had a successful career in college and in his final year of eligibility, went undefeated and was a national champion in his weight class. He is an icon in the wrestling world and in 2012 was inducted into the National Wrestling Hall of Fame and is now a highly sought-after motivational speaker.

Coach must have used a lot of favors to pull it off. He wanted Anthony to pump me up, and what a payback for my practical jokes the way he set it up.

All day on the designated Friday, whenever one of my teammates crossed paths with me in class or in the halls, he would intentionally avoid making eye contact and mumbled things like, "Hey, Willie. How's it going?" or, "Take it, easy man, we're gonna miss ya."

They all wore their best somber faces to be sure I took note and would be suspicious of their unusual greetings. I took the bait, hook, line, and sinker and became concerned that something bad involving me was coming down.

Coach Jarvis called my dad to let him in on the joke and asked if he could come to school for practice to add some realism to the prank. Coach told him the players were all in on it and based on what they had seen, they were pretty sure I thought I was going to be canned.

When Dad arrived, he faked a serious look on his face, and my eyes filled with tears. He played along and told me Coach asked him to come over for a meeting. I told him I didn't think I was in trouble, but I didn't know what was going on.

He rolled me into a small auditorium and there was Anthony Robles on the big screen with a big wide grin on his face. When he saw me, he yelled out, "Hey, Willie." Coach then let me in on the joke that I wasn't going to be cut from the team, and that they just wanted to set me up on Skype to listen to Anthony.

You could have knocked me over with a feather, it was so funny. They got me good! I couldn't believe every one of my teammates had gone along with the prank. No one had spilled the beans. Amazing!

True to form, Anthony had words of encouragement for me that also had to have meaning for the rest of the team. He spoke about the obstacles in his life he had to overcome and for us not to worry about our wins and losses. They were going to be what they were.

He encouraged us to be sure to enjoy our journey, and not be solely focused on winning a championship. If we have the ability to do so, great, but it's about the journey, not necessarily the results. He reminded us to work hard and strive to perform to our highest capabilities at all times, to never give up. Good results don't come without dedication, he emphasized.

Maybe his most meaningful comment was when he told us the most memorable moments we'll have won't be from the medals or the big matches, or the championships. Sure, we won't forget them, but our best memories will be the camaraderie and good times we shared with our teammates. His example was that even after all the years since he wrestled in high school and went on to win a national championship in college, he and his old high school teammates still get together each Thanksgiving to hang out and practice. It no doubt rejuvenates their memories. Proof that for him it actually is about the journey.

His words hit home hard for me. I'm a relationship person and I realized I was at a point where I was no longer enjoying the journey and was too focused on the end result – winning. I needed to get back to enjoying the journey. I was, after all, living a dream just being on a wrestling team.

I was in awe of Anthony and very impressed that Coach Boyd and the others thought enough of me to give me a boost in the way they had. Arranging for me to meet and speak with a star like Anthony Robles **as part of** a practical joke doesn't get any better for me. Talk about memories - I'll never forget this one.

My teammates' and coach's concern about my state of mind showed me that my wrestling had deeper implications than my just trying to get a win. I had become a source of hope, in a way, for the school. I was no longer known as the poor kid in a wheelchair, to be pitied; I was just the kid who was wrestling against long odds.

If I gave up on myself, I would be giving up on everyone else who believed in me. It was a heavy weight, but one I was willing to carry. I got my mind back on track and kept on working, convinced that my hard work and positive attitude would eventually pay off.

***

The high point of my junior year may have been a match I nearly won. I don't recall which school we were wrestling, but my match was very close. I had a chance to win and one or two good moves on my part could have closed the deal, but I lost. I was encouraged though, coming that close, as were my coaches and teammates. We felt I was going to break through at any time, and despite having lost the match, it was exciting to be so close and have a chance to win.

We were in a tournament the following weekend called the Jefferson County Tournament of Champions which we called JCTC. Before the tournament, they posted the match brackets on the gym wall so we all knew who we'd be wrestling against. When I looked at the brackets, I saw my first match was against the kid I had almost beaten the prior week. I was excited. I knew I'd get him this time - I had to!

Unfortunately, things didn't go my way and he beat me again. I was so upset-actually distraught. After the match, I sat with my hoodie pulled down over my face so the others wouldn't see me crying into it. *Why can't I win? Why did I have to keep on losing? Just one win and I'd get this monkey off my back!* I was so disappointed, being as close to winning as I thought I was, then getting whipped the way I did.

My coaches did their best to console me, reminding me it's all part of the process. They say that losing builds character, but I was tired of losing every single time I crawled on the mat. I still wanted to win somehow, some way, to prove to myself I could. *I had to win. I needed to win!* I couldn't keep letting these good opportunities slip away.

One of my teammates, a huge guy, Anthony Jennings, our captain that year and one of the nicest people I'd ever met, came up to me as I sat there feeling sorry for myself and said, "I've been exactly where you are right now, Willie. Trust me, it will get better. The fact that losing gets you this upset tells me you're going to get better. If you didn't care, you wouldn't be sitting here crying the way you are. I can see you want this very badly."

It was nice of him to talk with me the way he did, to show he understood and cared. It raised my spirits and also showed me how a good team captain should act.

A saying I've heard that I like and believe is, "Failure hurts for a short time but quitting hurts for a lifetime." Despite my failure to win, there was no way I would quit!

Brenda:
I was always so proud of the way Willie handled his responsibilities with the team. I doubt if many people could do what he did, and the way he went about it. Being on the wrestling team was a good diversion for him from his daily struggles with CP. However, at the same time, the wrestling itself increased his

frustrations and emphasized the debilitating effects of the CP.

But rather than taking it out on everyone around him, including his teammates, he turned his struggles and his efforts to overcome them into motivation for the team. What more could you ask of him?

As motivating as he was for those on his team, at home, life had its challenges for him and me. Even though he wasn't winning his wrestling matches, the majority of the time he spent with his teammates was in practice and training. That was the biggest source of his enjoyment. He loved working through the physical routines, being one of the guys, clowning around in the locker room - enjoying the camaraderie of his teammates.

By comparison, life at home isn't nearly as exciting. It never is. Teenagers, in general, are a lot to handle and Willie was no exception. When he was in a bad mood or a funk, it affected me too and I'm sure my bad days affected him as well. None of us is perfect. Life isn't easy no matter who you are. We got through our hard spots though, which more often than not revolved around his frustration about not being able to be more independent.

Those with disabilities have a much harder time than others with maintaining a positive balance in their lives. They are so dependent on others that they have little if any, independence. But independence is what teenagers live for. They want to experience life to its fullest. More often than not they learn the hard way.

One day a pharmacist asked me what it was like caring for a disabled person. I told him as a normal child gets older they get more independent of their parents and the parents get back more time for themselves. But when you're dealing with a disabled person that doesn't happen. It actually gets harder as they get older because you're still lifting and helping them get dressed and doing all of the other things you always do for them. But now they're heavier and as you get older, it's harder on you.

We argued at times because Wille would get frustrated that he couldn't lead a normal life. He just wanted to hang out with his friends when he wanted to. He was able to go out with them at times but just not at any time they called. His times out required careful planning. But teenagers get more mobile when they are able to drive a car, and he couldn't. He was stuck at home more than he wanted to be. He just wanted to be a normal teenager, but couldn't in many ways.

I would get frustrated because I wanted to help him but couldn't, so we were both frustrated about his situation. When people are frustrated with situations they can't change, they can get on each other's nerves. Willie was seeing his friends and others getting on with their lives in many ways, but his life wasn't changing much. It wore on us both, but we learned to deal with it.

As much as I hate the wheelchair, I've often wondered what kind of man Willie would be if he wasn't in it? I'm very proud of him being a godly man, even though he struggles with many things in his life, as everyone does. But he keeps trying and trying and you have to admire his perseverance.

The many limitations Willie has experienced in his life make his role as a motivator, both on his team and to others, pretty amazing. I believe whatever Willie chooses as a career or ministry he will always be a motivator to others. His outgoing personality is an asset and he is always focused on the objective of whatever he is undertaking at the time. He leads by example.

9

The Breakup—
The Change in Our World

For though the righteous fall seven times, they rise again,
but the wicked stumble when calamity strikes
—Proverbs 24:16

Willie:

A few years before I got to high school and began my wrestling career, I got a jolt! It had nothing to do with my physical challenges, but in a way, was possibly more devastating to me – my parents split up! It shocked me to my core.

At the time I was mainly focused on my own challenges, and while kids may sense tensions in family relationships, my parent's marriage ending is something that never crossed my mind. I was caught way off guard.

My dad and I had grown pretty close over time. He wasn't into sports like me, but he took me to events and wherever I needed or wanted to go. I realize now it had to be a financial and emotional strain for my parents to care for me the way they had for all those years. The expense of a special needs child is to a large extent mostly borne by the parents.

He was in good physical shape from working as a pipefitter, so he was able to lift and assist me despite my growing size as time passed. Where most kids would be walking, he'd be carrying me or pushing me in my wheelchair.

He didn't play sports with me very often since he wasn't a sports-oriented guy, so he mainly watched me playing with my toy action figures. I didn't care, though. He did his thing and I did mine.

Occasionally we would wrestle or horse around, or he'd run with me through the basement holding me like I was flying. Dad admitted to me and others that, in his own words, he stunk as an interactive father. But he was there when I needed him and I was able to entertain myself most of the time, anyway.

As I got older, I needed help changing my clothes, getting in and out of the bathtub or shower, and with other daily routines. He was there to assist me, which meant more to me than his playing games with me when I was younger. Dad wasn't like a run-of-the-mill dad, though, if there is such a thing. He was definitely cut from a different cloth, but we were still very close. *He knows who his daddy is*, as he would say about me. But all in all, he was a good dad and still is.

You wouldn't know he had a very checkered past, either. In his younger days, he ran with a motorcycle gang, *The Outlaws*. He wasn't a member per se but was classified as a "*hang around.*" It was one of the first steps toward eventually being granted membership in the gang.

He didn't like some of his duties in the gang, so after a while, he decided to get out and began to go to church. He heard that Mike Duke, the former president of The Outlaws was the preacher at Churchman Chapel, so he began going to services there. Dad is a simple, yet complicated, man.

∗∗∗

Mom and Dad met at Churchman Chapel. They had been married for eighteen years. Now they were deciding to divorce. They both had been married before, but neither had any children from their previous marriages.

That the three of us came to be a family at all was unlikely. But we *were* together and I thought we were doing very nicely until Dad dropped a bomb on Mom and me.

I say bomb because a few weeks before he told Mom he was leaving, he told me. As would be expected with this type of announcement, my world was turned upside down. It definitely put a huge weight on me being only twelve years old. Can you believe it? I didn't know what to do. I was just a kid.

I didn't play any sports then, so I wasn't known as an athlete with teammates or coaches for support. I wasn't known as a brainiac, so I didn't have the smart guys to hang around with. I was goofy, but I wasn't always goofing around, and I would joke around, but I wasn't always joking around. I wasn't part of a group and didn't belong to a big social network.

I felt lost like I was floating, and being disabled I couldn't get away from it. I didn't know what to do to cope. *Do I tell her? Would Dad maybe change his mind and stay?*

For weeks I struggled with what to do. *What would happen if I told her?* Under the strain, I looked for an escape and it's possible as a result I started acting up in school. I got into an argument with my teacher's aide, did some things I regret, and got suspended. That may have snapped me back to reality.

It made me realize I had to cope with the results of the situation since I couldn't change them. Mom would just have to take on helping me physically, as difficult as it would be for her. We had no other options.

It's easy to take for granted your parents will stay married, especially after they've been together for eighteen years and all you've ever known is them being married. It would be hard for any adolescent, especially one as dependent on others as me. Half of my support system would be gone.

I was sad when they split up and it hurt. I knew raising a child with disabilities was difficult enough and I dreaded the thought that I was the cause of their breakup.

Dad later told me he regretted telling me about their split-up before he told Mom. He said he was trying to protect me from the shock of it and to prepare myself for his moving out. He didn't want me to come home from school one day and find he was gone, so he thought his telling me before Mom was a good solution. In reality, it wasn't. I think it made it more difficult for me. In some ways, I felt I had betrayed Mom by not telling her, and I didn't like that feeling, either.

In the beginning, I missed Dad not being at home with us. I cried and often asked Mom to ask him to come home. But it was me wanting it all to go away not fully understanding adult relationships. Mom and I were both hurting, but we coped with it the best we could.

One day I hit a breaking point and tore apart the extra bedroom we used as a computer room. I didn't have another outlet for my anger or fear or whatever I was feeling at the moment, so I took it out on the room. I was just tired of it all. I think my tirade helped relieve a lot of my built-up tension and frustrations. It wasn't so good for the room though.

To further cope, Mom and I would have a "Willie" day every now and then when, if I was feeling blue, we'd do whatever I wanted for the day. It was a good relief to ease my pain. Nothing like goofing off to get your mind right!

Mom suggested I get some counseling to help me deal with my feelings. I did, but I didn't really need to, and the counselor agreed. I was no longer harboring any anger toward my dad and I was more concerned about what it all meant for Mom.

He always helped me physically and she is a small woman and I didn't want to be a physical burden on her. Mom subsequently cut her work hours, so she was home with me more, which oddly enough, resulted in our getting into frequent arguments. We were both still hurting. Her being home more may have been a reminder.

After a while, though, I adjusted and matured. Mom later mentioned to me that 85% of the parents of special needs children end up in divorce because the stress level is so high. I regret we weren't able to beat the odds.

I later learned my dad's father had run off and left him when he was only fifteen years old. When he asked his mother where his father was, she just told him that he wouldn't be coming home. It tore him up when it happened to him, and though he left Mom, and I suppose me, he hasn't disappeared as his father did and is still a big part of my life.

He and Mom have worked it out to where they take turns when possible to get me to where I need to go since I'm so reliant on others for transportation. He stops over at our house regularly and he and Mom seem to get along with each other pretty well, as time has passed. He still wants to be a part of my life, and I want him to be.

***

As often happens when couples get divorced, one or both remarry or have a significant other. Dad had a big wedding and remarried a woman named Janie after his and Mom's divorce was final. I was invited and went to the wedding. Since I was only twelve years old, I didn't have a strong opinion about it, one way or the other.

Actually, I probably didn't know how to feel about it. All I knew is it was a wedding and my dad was getting married, so I went. Mom was okay with me going. The whole divorce and remarry situation reminded me of an afternoon soap opera, although I couldn't change the channel to watch something else. It was real. We lived it!

I told Mom she should go to the wedding, too. She didn't think it was a good idea although she laughed when I brought it up. Crashing the wedding of an ex-spouse sounds like something from the *Jerry Springer Show* — maybe a good follow-up to the soap opera.

Brenda:

Although it's never one thing that leads to a breakup, the stress of caring for a special needs child may have led to ours. We were both working full-time; I was working more than forty hours per week because in my job I had nights where I was on call. Sometimes I'd be out till ten or eleven or twelve at night after working all day.

Every therapist gives their patient exercises to do at home, for which they need their parent's help. I became frustrated, so one day I spoke with Jamie, Willie's physical therapist, and told her I was finding it hard getting it all in. She said, "Brenda, you could work with a child like Willie twenty-four hours a day and it wouldn't be enough. You've just got to do what you can."

I tried not to take my stress out on Willie, but I did fuss at him a lot and I shouldn't have, but the stress has to go somewhere. It needed an outlet, but it wasn't fair to him.

One of the biggest problems caregivers have in dealing with those with special needs is that they can't get away from it. It's difficult to get one hour, one day, any time totally to yourself. There were many times I wished I could have had an entire day to myself, just to curl up and read a book or just to be able to clean the house from top to bottom. Not to have to worry about, "Mom, can you help me change my clothes? Mom can you help me get in the shower?" or "Mom, I'm hungry," or whatever the need of the moment is. You can't make the situation disappear – it's with you all the time.

Even now with Willie as an adult, he needs constant care. When he gets up in the morning, I help get him in his wheelchair. Sometimes I would help get him on his walker and we would take a walk down the street to Mom and Dad's house and back. Other times he'll do some exercises where he lays on the floor and does push-ups and such. He still likes to work out hard, so I take him out to the garage, but I have to lift him up on the rowing machine. He really works up a sweat when he's out there because he wants to – probably a carry-over from his wrestling days. Then he's soaking wet and I've got to put him in the shower. Afterward, he's hungry and wants something to eat. Half your day is over before you know it.

Sometimes I'd have to say, "Okay, Willie. Timeout. I need a shower," or, "I need some prayer time," or, "I need to do a few things myself." There were times when I just had to say no. Sometimes he would argue with me about it. He'd say, "but Mom, you knew I'd need all this help when you adopted me because I'm handicapped." As he's gotten older he understands and says, "Yeah Mom, do what you have to do. I'll be okay."

When mothers have babies, they say they sleep with one ear open. It's the same way with a special needs child, but it goes on much longer. I've listened for Willie for so long over the years that even now when he spends the night with a friend, I sometimes think I hear him calling in the middle of the night from his room.

When we first split up, Larry would take Willie on Tuesdays and then every other weekend. One day out of the blue he walked in and said, "I've decided I'm not going to take him anymore." I said, "Larry, you can't do that. I can't go it alone all the time." But he said he wasn't going to take him anymore and he meant it.

Suddenly, I didn't have any help from him. It was difficult for me to adjust to being a single parent with a special needs child. Before, Larry and I took turns with the lifting and bathing and all the other things that Willie needed help with. Suddenly it was all on me. I just cried, "Lord, help me get through this."

I knew the Lord hadn't abandoned us though, because one night after I had put Willie to bed I got down on my knees and I was praying by the couch in the living room and I felt the Holy Spirit come through the house like a whirlwind. I got very excited and had a vision. In it, I saw a black piece of velvet with candles lit on it and I knew every candle was a prayer. I got excited and jumped up and down saying, "the saints are praying, the saints are praying."

The next morning I didn't say anything to Willie, but he said to me, "Mom, you know last night, I was laying there sleeping and all of a sudden I woke up and the Holy Spirit filled my bedroom." I replied, "Wasn't that great?" and he replied, "yeah." I asked him what he did and he said he just laid there enjoying the feeling for a while and went back to sleep.

I was pleased that he felt the way he did and was comforted by the presence of the Holy Spirit. Some people think being a Christian is boring, but it's exciting!

Even though I felt the strength of the Holy Spirit and the Lord looking out for us we still had to plod on with life. Willie's therapy was still going on at the time and after about a year I thought, *Enough is enough.* I canceled his vision therapy and stopped his occupational therapy. He completed his speech therapy and we kept going to physical therapy. I just couldn't keep up with it all. Something had to give.

Financially, it was more difficult to stay ahead of things with Larry gone. Sure, he paid child support, but it's not the same as having another household income. My dad was always so kind when it came to money and helping others. He knew things were tight for us and when he asked if we were able to make ends meet I told him we were able to scrape by. Nevertheless, he gave us the money to pay off the mortgage on our house. He left nothing to chance when it came to Willie and me. We both loved him dearly.

When Larry and I decided to adopt Willie, we obviously never dreamt our marriage would end in divorce, or we wouldn't have considered the adoption. When it did, we had been married for eighteen years which is far longer than many marriages last. I wouldn't describe ours as a dream marriage, but we were happy enough. Sure, our lives changed a lot after we adopted Willie from what they were for the previous eight years, but all lives and marriages go through change. Life would be pretty darned boring if everything remained as is, forever.

But we were doing what we thought was God's will by adopting, so I suppose I may have thought He would have helped us through some of the rough spots every marriage endures, much less a situation like ours. Willie and I have now adapted and Larry and I get along okay and are even now playing music together at Church.

But our divorce may have been the single most life-changing event for me since the adoption because it forced me to be the single parent of a special-needs child, a situation which would have prevented my adoption of Willie, to begin with. After-the-fact events are often the most difficult to accept when we feel we didn't give them proper consideration beforehand. But at adoption time, wondering what would happen if Larry and I divorced never crossed my mind. We were following God's will.

10

My Other Family—
Surviving My Heritage

He will cover you with his feathers, and under
his wings, you will find refuge; his faithfulness
will be your shield and rampart.

—Psalm 91:4

Willie:
Many who are adopted know little about their birth parents. It's often better that way. That was not the case for me. Since my adoption wasn't through an agency but was arranged through our Church, it was open. Many knew who my birth parents were.

My physical condition probably related back to them, not genetically but because of their lifestyle and drug abuse. It's hard to ignore a physical disability as obvious as mine. What traits did I inherit from them, if any? I'll never know. All I can do is wonder.

When I had the courage to crawl onto a wrestling mat at a disadvantage to take on an opponent hovering over me, was it because of them, or in spite of them that I was able to rise above the obstacles they forced on me? Were they good people who simply hit a bad stretch? It's not my place to judge.

My birth mother, Trina Jones, who was only seventeen years old when I was born, already had another son. He was from a man other than my biological father and was two years old. Since I was adopted at birth, I didn't know I had any siblings until much later in my life.

Trina had another son after I was born, again, by another man other than my father. I have a sister, Sadie, who has the same father as me. In all, Trina had four children by three different men, so I have two half-brothers and a full-blooded sister.

I don't initiate or stay in contact with my half-brothers since we don't have much in common. They both live out of state in different parts of the country with their father's families. The last I heard, one of them lives in Arizona and the other in Nevada. I do have some contact with my sister, Sadie, who still lives in the Louisville area. She and I regularly speak on the phone.

My father was Bobby Broyles. Bobby was living with his girlfriend while he was having an affair with Trina when she became pregnant with me. After he and his girlfriend broke up and I had been adopted, he and Trina got back together and were married, and then they had Sadie.

Trina died in 2011. I was only 15 at the time. She was only in her early thirties but a drug addict. I was told she died from a drug overdose. I was invited to her funeral but decided not to go. It was probably good that I stayed away. However, now I feel some regret for not having gone. We weren't close, but she was, after all, my birth mother. I just didn't want to see her buried in the ground. It may have been awkward for me had I gone because I may have merely been a reminder to the other mourners of her past. I didn't like that idea.

At times someone's death is hard to understand, especially for an adolescent, and doubly hard for someone like me who isn't sure how they feel about all that had occurred between them.

While I didn't feel much remorse about her passing, I also didn't feel anger or have hard feelings about the challenges I face every day because of her drug use before and during her pregnancy. I suppose if I spoke to Dr. Phil or someone like him about it, they'd be able to dig down deep inside me and uncover the real reason I didn't want to attend her funeral. Perhaps it was that I didn't want to be around the person responsible for what happened to me. Or maybe I just didn't want to be the poster child for her troubled life. Who knows? It's over.

I didn't have much contact with her over the years, which is normal for adopted children as most have little information about their birth parents. Over time I did ask Mom a lot of questions about my past. Why was I adopted, and would I have been the way I am if Trina hadn't used drugs?

She even took me for a short visit with Trina once. I sat on Mom's lap and Trina approached and spoke to me. We showed her pictures of me, but I didn't open up and talk to her until the last five minutes or so we were there. It was weird seeing her because I am her spittin' image. We resembled each other so much it was obvious she was my birth mother.

When I felt I had enough, I looked up at Mom and said, "I'm ready to go," and we left. I'm normally an outgoing person, but I wasn't so much so during the visit. Personal feelings are hard to understand at times, but children often show their true unfiltered feelings. No telling what I was really thinking.

We obviously had no idea Trina was going to pass away just a few years after our visit, so I'm glad we went when we did. Mom always seems to know the right thing to do and a sense of when to do it.

Mom told me that when I was around two years old, Trina came to a Churchman Chapel service. Mom and Dad were up on stage with the rest of the Praise Team playing music. Dad spotted her in church right before Praise and Worship began, so he commented to a friend, "That's Willie's real mom, keep an eye on her."

Mom didn't know she was there because she's shy and tends to keep to herself, so she just went up on the stage and played her guitar. After the service, several members commented, "Did you see that blonde in the black dress crying? Boy, I was praying for her all through church."

They weren't aware she was my birth mother. Maybe she was begging forgiveness from the Lord for her actions. Maybe the other's prayers helped her find peace. Prayers never hurt. The Lord does listen. No one knew that better than the kind souls at Churchman Chapel.

Bobby, my natural father, also died at a young age, forty-eight, in 2016. He was suffering from an infection possibly caused by his own years of drug use. I didn't attend his funeral either, but I didn't know he had passed away. My sister, Sadie, didn't call me with the news, so the funeral was over with before I knew about it.

As I recount this story about my birth parents and their lives as I know it, I can't help but think how God rescued me from what would have been a horrible life had I not been put up for adoption at birth.

How would they have cared for me through the years if they were strung out on drugs at times? Would I have been able to go to therapy and have a family as kind as the Dukes babysit and help raise me? The obvious answer is, no.

Both of my natural parents died before I was twenty-one. What would have happened to me had I not been adopted? Would I have become a ward of the state and been institutionalized? I shudder to think how my life may have turned out. As it did, instead, I have been surrounded by love my entire life. What a lucky person I am. Praise to the Lord for rescuing me and praise to those who followed His will.

Brenda:
I can honestly say I don't hold any hard feelings or anger toward Trina for Willie's condition. I do recall wondering how someone could do something like that to another human being. She knew the risks to him because of her drug use. I know it was an addiction, but you can't use that excuse for all of your actions.

When we were considering his adoption, I prayed to the Lord to give me a sign that Willie would be okay and that we should proceed. He did and we went ahead and I've never looked back wondering if we had done the right thing. It hasn't been a walk in the park, but no one's life is.

Had Trina been truthful and not lied about her drug use when I visited with her the night before Willie was born, I may have walked away. Many people would have. But I had previously worked as a nurse in the NICU, so I was familiar with the equipment used on premature babies and all the possible complications of premature births. This gave me some comfort and confidence in our decisions. At the least, we made informed ones. Maybe this was one of the reasons the Lord chose us.

When Larry and I would go to the hospital, he was focused on how Willie looked. He'd say, "Oh, he looks so good." I, on the other hand, was looking at the equipment and monitors. I'd reply, "Oh, but this isn't good since they've increased this medicine," or, "his counts on the respirator don't look so good." I was putting my expertise to use.

It became an ordeal though because Willie was in the hospital for two months before we brought him home. You deal with circumstances like this one day at a time and one prayer at a time. We stuck with it though and went forward with Willie's adoption the same way we adopted the Lord's plan for him.

We brought our precious little baby home from the hospital right after Thanksgiving in 1995. What a wonderful present to celebrate the upcoming birthday of Our Lord and Savior.

I knew we were being smiled upon from above for accepting the challenge He put forth upon us. I knew our life would be different from that point forward and I was okay with it. I didn't know exactly how or when it would change and I was okay with that too. We were doing the Lord's work and he would provide all the strength and courage we would need to raise this baby boy in His image.

***

When I had held Willie in my arms the first time, I knew I was his mom. But one of my biggest fears was the thought of losing him back to his birth parents. At the time we were adopting Willie there was a court battle going on that was being covered by the national news. A woman had given up her baby for adoption and later when she and the natural father got married, they wanted their child back and fought for custody. By now the child was three years old. Unbelievably, they won the case and got the child. All the adoptive parents got were some visitation rights. That didn't seem right to me.

I thought how awful that would be for a young child to be taken from the only parents and family she knew and go to a family she had never known. And how awful for parents who had accepted another's baby into their life and raised them with love and devotion only to have them ripped from their arms. I was wary.

When Willie was in the NICU, Trina would go down and see him. I would see her name on the sign-in book. I was afraid she was going to change her mind and want him back.

When we met with our attorney about the adoption, the first thing I asked him was, "What are the chances that Trina could come back and try to take Willie away from us?" He replied, "Not in a commonwealth state," which Kentucky is, "When the parents sign over their rights, it's over."

His response helped ease some of my fears, but I wasn't as close to the Lord then as I am now, so I was still fearful of what may happen. Now I know God is in control.

The whole adoption process took almost three years because Willie's natural father kept dodging our requests to sign the necessary documents because he thought we were seeking child support. So I constantly worried we might lose Willie until the adoption was final.

The adoption was completed on May 7th, the National Day of Prayer that year, and I had much to pray for both in need and thanksgiving. We had to go to court to finalize his adoption and I'll never forget Willie sitting on my lap and the judge smiling at him and asking, "Willie, do you know why you're here?" And he replied, "Yes," as he patted my arm and said, "This is my mom," and "this is my dad," as he pointed to Larry. The judge signed the papers and Willie was officially our son. Praise the Lord!

Throughout his youth, Willie would ask many questions about Trina and his whole situation in general. He became curious at a very young age, and around age three or four, he asked me why he was adopted. I told him his mother gave him up because she couldn't afford to take care of him. That was a simple answer and for a child his age, it was enough at the time.

When he was six years old, his questions got more serious. He asked, "Mom, you and Dad have helped a lot of other people out who needed a helping hand. Why didn't you help her out?" I told him we didn't help her because we learned she was a drug addict and she would have spent the money on drugs. His quick response was, "So you mean I might not be like I am if she hadn't taken drugs?"

I thought for a minute and decided my response would be, "You were born premature, you may have gone through this anyway, but the drugs definitely didn't help." He accepted my answer at least for the time being. I didn't expect such probing questions from him at such a young age. I was surprised at how he put two and two together.

Later, around age nine he asked if he could see her. Evidently, his disabilities and the whole matter of adoption weighed on his mind at times, or maybe it was just his curiosity. Regardless, I decided to take him to see her.

I was hesitant at first, but I kept thinking teenagers can be rebellious and I didn't want him later looking for her simply because she was a mystery to him. I thought if he met her now, he wouldn't want to look her up later. I also felt it better to get it over with under my supervision sooner than later.

I made arrangements for us to visit and we went to her home. I knew he was mine because the adoption had been finalized years before so I was no longer worried about losing him.

I didn't quite know what to expect because years earlier Kathy Duke had gone to Trina's home to give her clothes for another baby. She said when she entered the house, there were three young girls sitting on a couch. Trina wasn't home at the time. There were three small babies playing on the floor—it was a filthy, horrible place. Being the kind woman she is, her heart ached for the children living there. She wanted to rescue them, but couldn't; what type of life would they have?

She went away saddened but said she couldn't help but thank God that He had delivered Willie from a situation like that. What would his life have been like if he had not been with us and spent as much time as he did with the Dukes?

Trina's home now was much neater than when Kathy visited years earlier. During our visit, Willie sat on my lap and as Trina approached he leaned back into me like he was pulling away from her. After she talked to him for a minute or two, he warmed up a bit, but he remained in my lap and wanted me close by.

They talked for about five minutes and then he turned to me and said, "Mom, can we go home now?" We were only there 15 or 20 minutes, but I knew whatever was on his mind about her, he was satisfied.

Before we left, she handed me a little black and white photo of her taken in one of those little photo booths where you got three pictures for a quarter. On the back, she had written, *I'm your Mama. I didn't say anything to her but thought, "You're not his mother, I am." I didn't keep the photo. Would you?*

It wasn't easy for me to take him to her not knowing the end result in advance, but it was the right thing to do for him, at the time. It gave him a perspective on his life that he knows was better off with Larry and me than with Trina and Bobby.

When Willie was fifteen, Trina passed away from a drug overdose. I thought how sad it was because she battled drugs for so long and they ended up wasting her life. I would see her one time and she'd be thin because of the drug use and another time she'd be heavier because she wasn't doing drugs.

She was actually in nursing school when she passed away. I can only imagine the battle she went through all the time trying to get and stay off drugs, but she was ensnared by them.

Willie didn't want to go to her funeral. He said he didn't want a bunch of strangers hugging on him. He didn't want that type of attention because of her passing. He says he now regrets not going. I would have taken him if he had wanted to go.

For someone like Trina who eventually succumbed to drug abuse, it wouldn't be rational to think she could have been with Willie 24/7 knowing she caused his disability. Willie needed to be surrounded by love, not a one-dimensional drug environment. He knows he's in a good place now. The Lord saw to it.

11

My Wake-Up Call—
My Deal With God

*Blessed is the one who does not walk in step
with the wicked or stand in the way that sinners
take or sit in the company of mockers.*
—Psalm 1:1

Willie:

Everyone experiences moments that shake them to their core and cause them to make changes in their life. Many can be attributed to God's intervention. Some listen and some don't. He can be subtle, like when He whispered in my parent's ears encouraging them to adopt me. The same is true for others when they read His word in the Bible and are saved.

I suppose He didn't think subtlety was the best approach for me to change some things in my life for the better. While many saw me as an example of the ability to overcome adversity and a role model to be admired and emulated, as a teenager I strayed from the straight and narrow occasionally, and it caught up with me in a nearly catastrophic way.

As a child, I was always going to church on Wednesday and Friday nights, and again on Sunday. My parents brought me there, so I didn't have an option to choose Christianity—I was told I was a Christian. It's natural for parents to raise their children in their religion, rather than having them choose one later on their own, and my parents were no exception.

I believe that someone with a physical disability may have challenges in their personal life because of the disability's limiting characteristics, their own self-confidence, or the general environment in which they live. At young ages, we don't always make the best decisions and can be tempted to fall in with those who give us attention or are popular themselves but aren't necessarily of the best character.

Fortunately for me, I had an outgoing personality and made friends relatively easily. Many are drawn to me because they don't expect my good sense of humor. My dad always said I was a peacemaker and peacemakers generally have congenial demeanors, which is a good attribute to have for making friends.

Once I began wrestling, everyone knew who I was and would talk to me. Then I made friends or acquaintances I could hang out with. Unfortunately, some of those I befriended may not have been the best people for me to be around.

In my teenage years, even though I was a Christian, I was doing what I wanted to do, not what I should have been doing. I was living the good life, partying, drinking with other guys and girls and doing the things that teenagers often do, but shouldn't. It all came into focus for me on my 18th birthday, during my junior year.

I was out with one of my friends who had just gotten a new BMW. It was pretty cool to be tooling around town in a new set of wheels, especially a BMW. I was sitting in the front passenger seat and there were two girls and another guy in the back. We had been out drinking and smoking some pot and generally doing things we shouldn't have been doing.

Though we were headed home, I shouldn't have been in this situation in the first place. It was stupid on my part.

My friend tried to beat a stoplight and make a left turn at a nearby intersection and misjudged the speed of the oncoming cars. We were about to be hit broadside on the passenger side of the car where I sat.

I saw the other car's lights coming right at me. In my mind, I thought for an instant I was going to die and on my birthday. It felt like it took forever, like slow motion, before the other car collided with ours. In that instant before the crash, my mind called out to God and told Him if He would get me out of this alive, I'd never do anything like this again, that I would change my life for the better, forever.

They weren't hollow words, I meant it. I knew I had placed myself in danger and I was doing everything I could to negotiate myself out of this predicament. I prayed it wasn't too little, too late. I knew I needed to be a better person. I was just hoping to get more time.

I heard the squeal of the brakes, but the oncoming car slammed directly into us, knocking our car sideways in the roadway. Naturally being too stupid to be wearing seatbelts, we were thrown around like rag dolls. The passenger door on my side was smashed all the way into my seat after taking the full brunt of the impact.

After the crash, I opened my eyes and realized I wasn't dead— so far, so good. The emergency responders had to pry open the door to get me out of the car. After I was out and checked over, I realized I had miraculously escaped without a scratch or even a bruise.

Other than having the bejeebers scared out of me, I was okay, a miracle of sorts. The policeman on the scene said he couldn't believe I wasn't seriously injured. He said and I knew I was one lucky kid.

I was also lucky in that if I had been injured and hospitalized, and gotten in trouble with the law, I would have been kicked off the wrestling team. I can't believe I put the one thing that meant so much to me in jeopardy. Talk about stupid. I took all of this as a message from God. He protected me and I was going to hold up my end of the bargain, and I have.

Now, when it comes to picking friends, I want to be a good man of God. I'm no longer worried about being popular. I saw where that got me. I want to be closer to Him and follow His will.

I felt my relationship with God wasn't as strong as it needed to be. I prayed and asked Him to remove whatever it was that was holding me back. I wanted to be closer to Him. Since some of my friends in the past have gotten me into trouble, although I was a willing participant, I knew I needed to be more careful about who I picked as friends.

Ironically, soon after I prayed, I got into an argument with a couple of my friends that I'd been very close to and suddenly they didn't want to talk to or be with me anymore. It made an impression on me that perhaps God heard my prayers and intervened. He does work in mysterious ways. He knew I needed a wake-up call. Now I choose my friends more wisely. My cousin, Chris, and I are very close. We understand each other and share ideas - the sign of good friends.

Some think Christianity is a like a rulebook, but it's not. There's a difference between religion and a relationship with God – they're two different things. If you get too caught up in the different religious denominations, it's going to lead to hurt and pain and a lot of division. Jesus is my best friend now.

Over the years, others have taken advantage of my kindness, so I've learned to be careful of whom I befriend. I'm like my mother. We are very open and giving. And we do whatever we can to help others. It doesn't matter if it helps me or helps another, I'll do it. I think some of the girls in my life may have used my kindness against me.

I do wish I had more of a backbone with people though. I enjoy being kind to others, to a fault and I wish I could turn down others sometimes, but still be nice. It's hard to say no though when so many others have helped me in my life. However, it's not usually those people who are doing the asking. It's those who want something from me.

I'm also not the type that looks for confrontation, being a peacemaker. I look for the good in people, not to dislike or harbor ill feelings toward others. I'm easy going. There's not enough room in my world for hard or negative feelings.

I don't understand it when it seems others are so unhappy all the time. I'm not wired that way. I'm always happy and happy that I am. My new philosophy is, *friends should be few, but well chosen.*

Now I look to Mom if I have questions about religion or Christianity. She's my guide. I'm a much better person now than I was before. If I struggle with temptation, I talk to her. She's self-admittedly traveled that road and knows the pitfalls.

Young people often want to keep things from their parents, they're afraid to confide in them. If I have something on which I need advice, I'll ask her about it and she'll help get me through it. She's my spiritual rock.

We've attended a number of different Christian churches and often choose those that are attended by our other family members. We like to worship as a family and support each other. We also like churches that offer programs and ministries of interest to me, which I feel I need.

Brenda:

When I learned that Willie had been in an accident, there wasn't much I could do after the fact. Emotionally you flip back and forth from anger at what they had done to the relief they weren't hurt. It shook him up emotionally at the time and has had a long-term effect on him. He felt vulnerable, not a pleasant feeling for anyone. He thought he was going to die because he saw the oncoming car and there wasn't anything he could do to escape. In some ways, I suppose you could describe it as being scared straight.

But God can take events like this and turn them into something good. I think in Willie's case He did. It made him re-evaluate his life, where he was going, what kind of friends he wanted to hang around with, and what kind of character he wanted to have. It changed his life for the better. He's become more spiritual and God-fearing as a result.

God just wants you to talk to Him. For me, it's not only important to get Willie's testimony out to help others, but I want people to know that there's much more to this walk than most Christians realize.

Willie and I have a good relationship and he confides in me on many topics, which I'm happy about. I don't have all the answers to life's questions, but we try to figure them out together. He's a good man and I'm proud to call him my son.

12

My Senior Year—
A Defining Moment

*I have fought the good fight, I have finished
the race, I have kept the faith.*

—2 Timothy 4:7

Willie:

My senior year began and I wondered, or maybe hoped this would be the year I broke through and could enjoy the fruits of all my hard work through the years with a win on the mat. I worked particularly hard to stay in good physical shape over the summer so I'd be ready for the season.

I was very pleased and humbled when I was elected a captain of the team, which motivated me in many ways. I was especially excited for the season to begin. It was a new start and things were already going my way!

Thud! My losing continued, but I actually felt I was getting better – some solace. Coach Boyd was the head coach that year. He and his wife had a new baby boy right before the season began, and he was also attending college, so he participated in practice when he could, and at the matches. Coach Jarvis ran the team most of the time when Coach Boyd was tied up with his other responsibilities.

Coach Jarvis was always working with me on technique, and he often introduced specific moves and holds for me to counteract my physical deficiencies. He coached me to stay low, wait, and then to spring at low angles at my opponent while trying to use the strong grip of my left hand as much as possible.

He thought I had the upper body of a 160-pounder and the lower body of a 90-pounder, so he wanted me to use my strong grip to get someone in a cradle or a power half hold so I could turn them to gain an advantage in a match. He believed that was my best chance to win. It may not have always worked out, but we both felt it was a good strategy and continued to use it.

I was excited the new moves were improving the quality of my matches but also disappointed the referee wasn't able to raise my hand as the winner at the end. I was earning more points in my matches, which was helping our team totals, but I wanted to enjoy the sweet taste of victory.

I had grown tired of crawling across the mat at the end of each match as a loser to congratulate the coach of the opposing team. I would sometimes lie awake at night strategizing in my mind what I needed to do to win. It helped me deal with my frustration, but I surely didn't want to be known as the "No-Win Kid," especially after being made a captain of the team.

While my teammates knew my personal story, the wrestlers and coaches from the opposing teams most likely didn't know most of the details, so while I wasn't looking for pity for just being out there, I wanted to gain their respect too by winning.

The season progressed with moderate team success. It was more of a team rebuilding year than a championship one, but it was exciting to be working and improving and competing.

The year rolled on until near season-end which would feature Senior Night. Most high school and college sports have a special night or day in which each senior is given special recognition. The athlete is usually accompanied by one or both of their parents who join them on the field or floor. Their mothers are usually presented with a bouquet of flowers. In our ceremony, the wrestler receives a plaque commemorating their participation.

The entire week of practice leading up to Senior Night, I

was very nervous. *What would it be like to win on this night? I dreamed.* What a stage that would be. There was no one else on my team in my weight class, so I knew I would wrestle.

One of our scheduled opponents that night had to cancel, and the one person I would have wrestled had beaten me a number of times before, so my odds of winning may have improved. So instead, we wrestled against a team from Pleasure Ridge Park High School, a much larger school than ours.

I knew mine was going to be one of the last matches of the night and I focused my mind as I always did, but this time it felt different. I knew this was one of the last chances I had to make an impact. I had wrestled over 100 times in my career without enjoying a victory, but that was then and this was now. I had to win this one!

The entire week leading up to the match I worked as hard as I could to improve my game. I worked every way I knew how to get stronger and faster—I felt prepared.

Senior Night arrived as planned. Looking back, the entire night was almost surreal to me. Leading up to the event, I had a very confident feeling that I was going to win my match regardless of who I wrestled. I don't know why.

It definitely played out oddly with our scheduled opponent having to cancel only to be replaced by another much larger school. The fact that I had lost a number of times to my originally scheduled opponent to be replaced by a wrestler from a different school whom I wasn't familiar with added to the unusual circumstances surrounding the night.

Before the matches, our team was waiting in the tunnel for our grand entrance and with a spotlight shining on the mat, and the music blasting, I closed my eyes and thought, *This is the last time I'll ever wrestle in front of our home crowd. I have to do something with this.*

We made a grand entrance into the gym amidst the normal Senior Night hoopla and warmed up for the crowd, who were screaming and cheering us on. We lay down together in the middle of the mat and held a team meeting without the coaches. We said the Lord's Prayer as we always did, and broke our huddle after we placed our hands together and yelled, "1-2-3, Bulldogs!"

We exited to the hall leading to the gym where we worked on psyching each other up. But I wasn't listening to the others, I was in my own world I was so focused. I was still thinking, *I have to do something here.* I thought about how a wrestling match is just six minutes, three two-minute periods, which can define your life. Would this be mine?

We returned to the gym for all of the typical ceremony connected with Senior Night, and Dad was there to escort me across the mat. Mom had to work and sadly couldn't be there to enjoy her well-deserved attention and receive her bouquet of flowers. I got a special award for being the only senior to have wrestled all four years, an unusual feat for someone like me. Then it was time to get down to business. I didn't know yet who my opponent was. It was unusual not to know in advance, another oddity for the night.

The team captains went to the middle of the mat for a coin toss. The winner gets to choose which weight class they want to begin the matches. Our coaches told us if we win the toss, to begin with the heavyweights. We won, so my match would be the last one since I was in the lightest weight class.

Finally, after what seemed like an eternity, it was my turn. I had drawn one of their female wrestlers. I had never wrestled her and didn't know her, nor her, me. I could see she was tall and lanky. I didn't feel her height would present a significant obstacle to me because opponents with longer legs usually made a bigger target for me to go after and grab. The shorter stocky ones normally were more difficult for me to handle.

Our team was beating our opponents pretty handily throughout the evening, which fueled our confidence and buoyed all of our hopes for my match. There was a good feeling in the gym. When my match was about to begin, my teammates helped me out of my wheelchair as always and I crawled to the center of the mat. My heart was pounding, my teammates were chanting my name. I was all hyped up and ready to go!

My opponent, Sydney Smith, met me in the center of the mat in her red and black singlet, her school colors. She was tall and angular with an athletic build you would expect on an experienced wrestler. I was not taking her lightly. She had survived in the wrestling environment in a big school program.

She stood and studied me, as she crouched over in the neutral starting position, as I was on my knees not being able to stand. The referee blew his whistle to begin our match and I dove for her lower legs, the technique I had been taught and had been using for some time, and was able to grab one. Coach Jarvis shouted, "Drive to it, Willie. Get your balance," as she struggled to free herself. "Trip with your other hand, Willie!" he barked.

I tried, but I couldn't reach it as I struggled to hold onto her foot and leg. She struggled to free herself by pushing down on my head. "Back to your base," Coach urged as the referee blew his whistle to signal a stalemate.

We returned to our starting positions facing each other, me on all fours and she once again hovering over me. The referee blew his whistle to resume and I dove for her legs. She was smart and had wised up to my technique and jumped away to avoid my reach while grabbing my back and jumping on top of me. She was awarded two points for a takedown - easy points for her. Darn!

Coach yelled, "Up, up! You've got to get you a base! Back to your knees, Willie!" I rose to my knees with her holding on, but she lunged forward to knock me off balance and I couldn't maintain the position holding up both of our weights. I fell back to the mat. I rose again with her behind me. I then dove forward hoping she would lose her grip, but she didn't and held on.

I tried to rise up using only my upper body, but she lunged forward again knocking us both down. I still couldn't break her hold. She was a good and worthy opponent. Coach continued to shout instructions as he did in every match. My teammates chanted, "Wil-lie, Wil-lie!" for encouragement. My mind swirled trying to figure out a strategy for my next move. She was tough and smart. If I was going to pull this off, I needed to call on every skill I had.

As I struggled to free myself, she hopped from one side of my back to the other to offset any leverage I was gaining with my own movements. She was both crafty and nimble, and it neutralized any advantage I had in upper body strength. I kept trying to raise myself up so I could roll over, but my lack of leg strength betrayed my efforts. She hopped over me once more.

She wasn't able to roll me into a vulnerable position, so she eventually broke her hold and stood as I crawled to a better position. I was awarded an escape point. My confidence soared, despite her being ahead by a point, because I could tell I was hard for her to handle, but I still needed to figure out a strategy to offset her moves, and quickly.

"Circle to her, circle to her!" Coach once again shouted. She placed her hand on my head to hold me back from leaping at her, but I was able to lunge forward enough to grab one of her legs around the back of the knee and pull her down. I was trying to hold her down as best I could to neutralize her and keep her from scoring more points.

"Drive, drive!" Coach screamed. "Got to get back to your knees, Willie!" I held onto her leg, but she was pushing down on my head to keep me from rising up. The whistle blew to end the period. She was ahead 2-1. I felt I could have done better, but I was confident in my position.

I got a few seconds to catch my breath as Coach motioned to me to begin the second period on top which is not a strong position, but because of my physical limitations, was one I was forced to use. It was just another obstacle I had to overcome to win.

"Willie!" Coach shouted, "look for a cradle!" his final instructions as the referee signaled for us to take our positions. (A cradle is a hold in which you grab the neck of your opponent with one arm and wrap the elbow of your other arm behind their knee.) She knelt on her hands and knees on the mat and I assumed the position from behind and wrapped my arms and hands around her waist.

She immediately jumped to her feet, which I couldn't stop as I was stuck on my knees, as Coach shouted, "Cradle right there, cradle right there," as I struggled to maintain my hold. I failed and fell to the mat as she flipped me and jumped on my back and grabbed me around my chest. The referee signaled a reversal, for the change in our positions, for her and two points. I was down 4-1. *I need to put on some moves to get some points, or this match is going to end up like all my other ones,* I thought.

"Get back to your base!" Coach shouted again. She struggled to control me, but when she realized she wasn't able to roll me over because of my upper body strength, she let go to try a different move. As a result, I was awarded another escape point and was now down 4-2.

We were face to face and once again I had my chance to dive for her legs. The home crowd was cheering for a takedown. We both had scored points early, which was good but I couldn't afford just to be trading points. I was still behind.

"Get your knees back under you," Coach blurted at me. She leaned in and pushed down on my shoulders to keep me at bay from being able to dive for her legs, but as she reached in further to grab my waist, it gave me an opening and I grabbed her leg again and held on. The crowd now cheered even harder for me.

She tried to flip me over to free herself, but I maintained my hold. *If I could get behind her back, I would win two points, but I would have to be in control to do so. If I could cover her hips I would also earn two points,* I rationalized. I pulled it off and was awarded a takedown and two points. My confidence rocketed. I thought to myself, *I've got this match, I've got this match! I can do it!*

"Drive, drive, Willie!" Coach shouted me back to the task at hand. "Drive into it!"

Again, she pushed my head down to keep me from gaining any leverage. I strained to rise to my knees a few times, but my weak and tiring legs betrayed me each time. I'd have to rely solely on my upper body strength if I was going to win this match, but I was determined to do so. Nothing was going to stop me!

I clamped onto her leg like a vise and I wasn't about to let go. She tried to rise up and I was able to reach around and grab her other leg – just the break I needed! I held both of her lower legs as she tried to crawl out of my hold. She fought and squirmed and was able to free one, but I held onto the other. My confidence soared. I knew I could do this!

She pushed against my head to try to gain some leverage to free her leg from my hold, but I refused to let go. I called on all my strength to hold on and my body responded. Then I used my stronger left hand to reach in and pull her closer, which decreased her maneuverability. She no longer had the advantage of using her legs and we were solely matching upper body strength. Now I had the advantage. *I can win this battle!* I thought to myself.

I reached for and grabbed her around her waist and I could feel my biceps bulging from the strain as I secured my grip. She struggled to free herself by attempting to crawl out of my hold, but I didn't let her escape as I concentrated on trying to secure a cradle hold. It is a very effective move against an opponent as it is very difficult to break and effectively neutralizes them if they aren't able to do so. "Hips up, Willie. Hips up!" Coach screamed.

"Don't let her go, Willie!" my teammates also shouted to me, which would have given her an escape point. "You've got eighteen seconds!" I held on and the period ended and we were tied 4-4. I was exhilarated to be in a position to win, but I still had to get it done.

At this point, we were both exhausted which was evident in our postures and we both struggled to regroup before the final period – the one they say is won by the wrestler with the biggest heart. My coaches and teammates continued to shout their encouragement. It was music to my ears. It wasn't often I made it to the final period in a match, much less be in a position to win.

After watching me wrestle for years without beating someone head to head, they may have sensed this could be the night, and they were revved up. I never felt more alive than I did at that moment and it gave me the boost I needed to begin the third and final period. *Lord, give me the strength to get through this,* I prayed.

My coaches signaled me to again begin the period in the top position. I'd have to be ready for one of her nimble moves to free herself and gain another easy escape point. My coaches shouted for me to continue to go for a cradle hold. I knelt over and held her around her waist as the referee blew his whistle to begin.

He did, and we both bolted and fought for position like a couple of crazy warriors. She tried to rise up and I had to release my grip with my right hand to brace myself to keep from falling to the mat and getting pinned. She lowered her head, but I was able to shift my body to be able to reach under her arm and grab her left leg which allowed me to gain control of both her left arm and leg at the same time. It was a nifty move for me at an opportune time.

"One more minute, Willie! One more minute!" my teammates shouted. I knew I could hold on for another minute, but I knew it would feel like the longest one of my life. I was in the dominant position and knew I had to maintain it in order to win the match. There was no way I was going to relinquish my hold, but I knew my opponent wasn't finished yet, either. *Please Lord, help me do this*, I prayed as my adrenaline surged to assist.

"Keep your cradle. Keep your cradle!" Coach screamed. She struggled to rise and free herself, but I could sense she knew she was doomed because it was too late in the match for her to overcome her dilemma.

"Fifty seconds, Willie!" Coach shouted the time remaining, which helped focus my attention, so I didn't get caught up in the drama of the moment. He also knew I needed to hear his reassuring, but commanding voice. I tightened my grip as much as I could with whatever energy I had left and I knew she wouldn't be able to free herself.

I felt her pause and relax for a second as if gathering her strength and I sensed, *here it comes*. She then called on every last bit of struggle she had left in her, because that's what wrestlers do, warriors to the end. She raised a leg to attempt to shift her weight to gain some leverage by changing my center of gravity, but I was entirely focused on maintaining my hold. My muscles were screaming, but they held.

"Thirty seconds, Willie!" Coach shouted, above the din of the screaming fans. "Keep pulling. Keep pulling!" as I clenched my hands together as tight as I could to keep her from breaking my hold. The referee kept circling around us knowing this titanic struggle was nearing its end and every point won was critical to both wrestlers.

If I let her get free, she would gain a point and I couldn't let myself lose that way, not after having come this far. She continued to fight and fight some more to free herself. She knew what she had to do.

The fans were now in a frenzy chanting my name and cheering me on because time was running out and they sensed I had a good chance to win. Oddly, some of the opposing fans were also cheering for me. My story of struggling to win was well known in the wrestling world as well as the community.

"Twelve seconds, Willie!" Coach shouted. *Please Lord, let this happen*, I prayed again. *I'm so tired, I can't go overtime!*

I held her in the cradle and the referee began waving his hand, signaling two back points for me with less than ten seconds to go and a 6-4 lead. Finally, the horn sounded to signal the end of the match, and we broke our holds.

Had I really won? I was stunned. The referee raised his right hand with a big smile on his face formally signaling that I was the winner as my teammates and the crowd went crazy. *Thank you, sweet Jesus!* Bedlam ensued in the gym.

I was numb. I was so exhausted I could barely move. I was both physically and emotionally drained, but also exhilarated. I managed to gather enough strength to rise up on all fours to my knees for the customary handshake between opponents and she was very gracious under the circumstances. I could tell she knew what it meant to me.

Oddly, the referee even moved in to congratulate me and the opposing coaches came out to the center of the mat to greet me as well. At that moment, the match was a blur to me. It was like my whole previous wrestling career was suddenly erased. It felt glorious! Where was I? I was in a daze in a very unfamiliar territory – a winner!

I had finally beaten an opponent in a match and did so in grand style with a clinching cradle hold, the strongest one in wrestling outside of a pin, and had held her scoreless in the final period to boot, an exclamation point to my already exciting win!

I crawled to the edge of the mat and my teammates immediately piled on top of me. They shouted, "Way to go, Willie. It's been a long time coming! Happy for you to get that win."

I replied, "I know. It took too long." It was an emotional moment for all of us, including my coaches. Coach Jarvis and I embraced and he told me how awesome it felt for me to win.

The crowd meanwhile continued to stand and cheer. I was the winner and I enjoyed their show of appreciation. It really put wind in my sails! I started to crawl off to my wheelchair but my teammates said, "No," and lifted me to my feet to move me from the mat. I had won and they decided my crawling away just wasn't right!

Though they carried me from the floor, emotionally I was floating. No one could ever take this moment from me! No more wondering if or when I'd win. I did it! The monkey was off my back and it ignited a flame in me I didn't want to see extinguished. The Lord had smiled on me that day. He made it one of the best days of my life!

> *The Lord has done it this very day;*
> *let us rejoice today and be glad.*
> —*Psalm 118:24*

***

It took a little time for the glow of winning to wear off, but a few days later we got back to business and were preparing for the year-end regional tournament. *Did I have a chance to win again?* I wondered. The individual winners get to move on to compete in the Kentucky state tournament so I was excited to see if I could pull off another win and get to move on to the ultimate stage.

The regional is a double-elimination tournament but the competition is at a very high level and no one wants to go home a loser.

During the entire week following my win, many were texting me saying I was going to win it all, trying to pump me up. It was nice for them to be happy for me, but I told them I wasn't thinking about the win because it was in the past. I was focusing on what lay ahead of me – the regional. That was my goal.

I was worried about the regional, so I was trying to get my head right. It was a difficult week leading up to the tournament because the press was all over with their cameras because of my win the week before. They had been watching me during the season, but now had good material for their big stories.

Reporters were constantly in our locker room and it was distracting and hard to get in the right mindset with cameras being constantly stuck in my face. Some of the members of the press even wanted to attach a microphone to my tee shirt. I don't know what they thought they were going to hear. Their questions went on endlessly with them following me wherever I went. I wasn't expecting this kind of attention.

The morning of the tournament could only be described as crazy. I felt bad that my teammates also had to endure the distractions of what was going on around me.

My first match was against a kid from Western High School. He wasn't that strong, but things got off to a bad start for me. As instructed by my coaches, at the beginning of the match as he approached me, I dove immediately for his ankles, hoping to grab on and pull him down near me so I could use my upper body strength to my advantage.

As I dove he bent down lower than I expected, so I missed them. He had put both of his arms down to block me and was able to get them under me and used my momentum to roll me over on my back. Now I was in trouble. He was savvy and he pinned me in the first period. I hated losing, but it was a double elimination, so I still had another chance.

I now had a long wait before my next match, so I had a lot of time to think. I was down after my quick defeat and my practical side thought, *just one more match and all of this is over. I won't have to worry about losing any more. It's going to be over.* I think I was actually happy about it. I was going to try my best to win, of course, so I could continue on to the state tournament, but in my head, it was more like, *one more match and it's over* - odd thinking for me.

But when they called my name to come to the mat for my next match, my competitive spirit kicked in and I realized, *Hey if*

I don't win, this is it for me. No more, *I'll get them next time,* or, *I'll come back next year.* This could be it. I wasn't ready to concede anything yet.

The kid I was to wrestle was from DeSales High School, a small all-boys private school in Louisville. My teammates circled around me, as they always did and encouraged me to work hard and to be sure I didn't give my opponent any easy points. There was a lot of chatter, but I wasn't listening to it. I was focused on winning, hoping this wouldn't be the end of my wrestling career.

When the match began, I dove for his legs. But he was too quick and was able to get around me. He wasn't able to roll me over because I was too strong. I fought hard for position, but he was able to pick me up by my legs, tilt me on my neck and roll me over in one quick move. Then he pinned me and the match was over in forty seconds. I was devastated. A wall of emotion swept over me like a tsunami.

I wasn't able to anticipate my reaction to it all in advance. I couldn't have known how I was going to feel – happy that it was over, or sad, but I suspected I would be upset. But the finality of it all slapped me unexpectedly in the face. Losing is hard, no matter what's at stake.

I shook my opponent's hand, and his coaches', as is appropriate, while maintaining my composure. I turned and my entire team was just staring at me, not knowing how to react - what to say or do. In that moment of hesitation and uncertainty, I broke down. We got into a huddle and I was crying and they were trying to console me with, "We love you, Willie."

Surprisingly, the entire crowd gave me a standing ovation. They knew my story and what wrestling meant to me. The officials, knowing I had wrestled for four years and this was my final match, didn't call for the next one right away, as they normally would in order to keep things moving, until I had exited the mat. It was a classy move and I appreciated their respect.

My teammates and I went behind the bleachers for a private moment. We were all together and they asked me what I wanted to do. I was distraught and they wanted to help but didn't know the right thing to do.

A chapter in my life had come to a screeching, undeniable end. Predictable, sure, but it hurt anyway. I went from the high of highs the week before when I won, not knowing how to react to that success, to this week with my wrestling career quickly coming to an end. It was a lot for me to deal with.

For some reason, I don't know why I wanted to take off my singlet. I just didn't want to wear it anymore, no good reason. One of my teammates went to our locker room to get my street clothes and I hurriedly changed. I was still hurting when Coach Jarvis approached me to attempt to console me.

We embraced for maybe two minutes. I could tell he felt my pain. He pulled me close and whispered in my ear. "This isn't it for you, Willie, you're not done here. Wrestling is a small part of what you were put here on earth to do. This isn't the end, it's the beginning. You are much bigger than the sport of wrestling. You are here to help others. You are going to do some great things with your life. You now have to decide how you're going to do it."

His words helped soothe the ragged edges of my emotions. My teammates put me in my wheelchair and Coach wheeled me from the gym.

Tristan, my friend, took it especially hard when I lost. He said he felt it coming. After all, it was the regional, but it hurt just the same. It was hard for him to see me break down and cry afterward because I rarely, if ever, cried which he knew from hanging out with me for so long. He knew I was hurting so he fell on top of me to console me.

He said it broke him that night. He also said that even though I lost my match and my wrestling days were over, he knew I'd always be there rooting for him. In friendship, we often have to witness both the good and the bad, together. Suffering through things together allows friendships to grow even deeper.

The day wasn't a total loss for me, though. After all the matches, I received the Most Outstanding Wrestler Award from the tournament officials, which was quite an honor. Obviously, they appreciated what I had attempted and accomplished in my wrestling career at Fairdale, which had now drawn to a close.

***

In the aftermath of my wrestling career, I received some unexpected recognition in the area. I got a nice letter from the Louisville Metro Council and they gave me an award for my dedication to the community. I'm not sure exactly what I did to earn it other than bringing some national attention to Louisville, but I appreciated it nonetheless. I'm sure being on the news and in the papers stirred some interest in the area.

One of my fun recognitions was when Fairdale Pizza, a sports-related restaurant, had a mural made for their restaurant of Fairdale High School wrestling and I was featured on it. Fairdale is an area of about 8,000 residents, but it meant as much to me as if it was hanging in Times Square in New York City. Everyone appreciates being honored by the local folks, but there was even more to come.

Brenda:

Willie obviously felt more pressure to win in his senior year. When I found out he had won on Senior Night, I was disappointed that I missed it but was so proud of him that all of his hard work and patience had paid off.

Willie immediately began receiving awards and other recognitions from local organizations, not only through his high school but he also received an award from the Aldermen of the area Metro Council. Everybody wanted some of Willie! He was an inspiration to everyone.

A reporter asked me how I felt about Willie getting the award. I said to him, "I'm just so proud of him. I'm just so proud of him." I couldn't think of anything else to say. That said it all. His ship had come in and was now sailing off to who knows where?

Struggling for points (Angie Matos Photography)

In control. (Angie Matos Photography)

One more period. (Angie Matos Photography)

I won! It feels great. (Angie Matos Photography)

13

In the Spotlight

For those who exalt themselves will be humbled,
and those who humble themselves will be exalted.
—Mathew 23:12

Willie:

Immediately after I had won, I was thrust into somewhat of a spotlight with reporters and other news people wanting to interview me or tape me going through my practice routines or whatever new angle they thought would generate any interest from their audiences. I thought it would end when I lost in the regional tournament and wouldn't be going to the state tournament.

However, I was wrong. My story was still news, most likely because I had only won the one match. I wasn't totally surprised because throughout high school news crews were around me occasionally, most likely because of the CP angle. The coverage afterward got revved up when the Louisville Courier-Journal returned for a follow-up story from a week earlier.

They had run an article about me being a disabled wrestler at Fairdale High who hadn't won a match but kept pushing on. They spent a lot of time with me through my high school career, so I was very familiar with them. Ironically, they ran the article a week before I won so they came back to follow up and I was headline news as *Willie Burton has his best match on his very last match at home and wins.*

The media loves this type of local interest good news. So much of what they normally cover is bad news or sad stories. Many newspapers around the state and outside were now writing about me and my story, even USA Today. I was a celebrity of sorts, I suppose.

My biggest media exposure came with ESPN. Unbeknownst to me, and perhaps to others, they had been quietly following me since I was a freshman and managed to work under the radar. They may have thought I was the ultimate human interest story in the making to have followed me for so long and to have invested so much time and effort, not to mention money, in me.

After I won, they came out of the background and said they were ready to do a documentary on me. You couldn't find a better story. All that losing and then my winning my very last match before the home crowd on Senior Night. It played out perfectly for them. No wonder they jumped on the opportunity to do a segment on me on their E:60 program.

They contacted my coaches at school and said they could turn this story into something very cool. The week after I got my win, Coach called me into his office, just the other coaches and me, and said, "We've got some really big news for you. ESPN wants to do a documentary on you."

At first, I was so surprised I didn't know how to react or what to think. I thought they may have been kidding because after my win and my story had been in the papers and on the news, I had been joking with my teammates the very same day about how cool it would be if I was mentioned on Sports Center on ESPN.

The next thing I knew my coaches were telling me ESPN *was* going to do an entire documentary on me. *Huh? Was this another payback joke by the team for one of the many practical jokes I played on them?* I thought. I wondered if the coaches knew what I had said to my teammates, so I told them I was only joking. They said, no, it was true. Holy Cow! I was going to be on ESPN! What a thrill.

For me, it was truly a very cool indescribable experience. We had to recreate practice scenes and the like for the cameras, which felt odd and in some ways like acting. Fortunately, they were able to use some real film which had been shot by WAVE Channel 3 in Louisville which had previously traveled with me to practices and tournaments.

The ESPN crew was with me non-stop for the next six months, but the documentary was only fifteen minutes long. I was always comfortable with the media and didn't have any issues with them. Mom and I enjoyed seeing how they went about their jobs. Behind the scenes isn't as glamorous as what's seen on the screen.

A funny story about the ESPN crew was that sometimes I would get in my walker and walk down to my grandpa's house a few blocks away. The film crew wanted to show how I worked to strengthen my legs and was taping me walking down the street. I could feel my shorts getting loose as I walked and I was sure they were going to fall down. I couldn't grab them because I was holding onto my walker to support my weight, so I kept walking.

Sure enough, they fell down. I'm out on the street being filmed with my shorts down around my ankles. It was hilarious. I yelled, "Don't put that in." They joked and said it would definitely go in. It didn't and I was happy. It was funny, but the whole world didn't need to see it!

The E:60 segment was outstanding. Its title is WillPower. What a catchy name - you can imagine I liked it! It told my wrestling story very well. It was narrated by Dan Gable, the famous NCAA and Olympic wrestler who won 180 straight matches and lost only one, compared to me, who lost over 100 matches and won only one. The gist of the story was that we were both wrestlers and therefore champions in our own way. I was honored to be compared in any way to such a historic figure in wrestling.

In addition to my being interviewed, the segment included my coaches, my teammates, and Mom and Dad. It also showed much of the match I won. What a special thank-you to my teammates and coaches who had my back and supported me all those years to have a video they could show their children and grandchildren of what they had done for someone less fortunate. A life lesson for everyone, and yes, they were on ESPN too!

I couldn't have been more pleased with the way it turned out. Many groups have shown it to motivate others to help overcome adversity in their lives. I owe ESPN a genuine debt of gratitude for what they did for me.

Overall, they were great to work with, especially Dan Lindberg, the producer. The whole process wasn't as big of a hassle as we thought it may be. They were all very professional and knew how to go about their work. I didn't actually like being filmed, but I did enjoy talking to the crew members. They had a good sense of humor and were fun to work with. It was great.

My only regret was when they swooped in on me immediately after I lost my last match to catch my reaction. I know they had to do their job trying to get the emotional side of the story. I was sitting in the corner crying with all my teammates and they asked me how I felt. It was pretty obvious how I felt. I was crushed. Actually, my story was probably more compelling by the fact that I lost the match following my only win, rather than following it with another win.

Brenda:

We enjoyed our time with the guys from ESPN. We had similar senses of humor. Dan Lindberg, the producer, told us we were down-to-earth people and he enjoyed working with us.

Overall, all of the news coverage and the subsequent ESPN documentary was somewhat overwhelming for us. We couldn't have anticipated the public's reaction to Willie's victory. It was almost like an avalanche.

But we were living with his disability every day, so his win while it was exciting for him and all of us, it was just that, a moment of excitement and reward. While we all took joy in his accomplishment, his disability didn't disappear with his losing streak ended. Now life just felt different, but better.

The subsequent publicity did allow his story to be told to groups and others which they often used for motivational purposes. That was very rewarding and helped ease the strain of all of the hardships Willie and his support groups dealt with for so long. Others were able to benefit from the example of his story. One of his goals is to be able to inspire others to persevere through any hardship.

He was especially pleased when a young person who had to endure hip surgery like him called him from Hawaii. He encouraged him and told him he could do it because he had, too. One-on-one motivational discussions are very rewarding.

The ultimate outcome of the news and media coverage is it told Willie his story is worth telling to help others and it gave him a platform from which to tell it.

14

More Challenges—
Finding the Right Partner

*God said: "If you never felt pain, how would you
know I am a healer? If you never had a trial, how
could you call yourself an overcomer?"*
                                    —*Author Unknown*

Willie:

If you think dealing with the physical issues of CP is difficult, you should try dealing with the personal relationship ones. Relationships with members of the opposite sex are something many often wonder about when one of the members has a physical disability. My situation was no different.

I wasn't always pursuing a relationship with someone. I'm not one of those guys who had to have a girlfriend all the time. At the same time, I wasn't avoiding girls, either. If one showed an interest in me, I would pursue it. There was no sense in subjecting myself to unnecessary rejection. If it worked out, it worked out. If it didn't, it didn't.

Dating a special needs person can be difficult and presents its own challenges, as would be expected. For example, my mom would have to drive me on a date, which usually meant to a girl's house to hang out or to hang out at my house. It wasn't the best arrangement for courting. No guy wants his mom to have to drive him on a date, but it was unavoidable under the circumstances.

My first steady girlfriend was when I was a senior and she, a freshman. We met at school. We started out as friends on Facebook, talked at school, texted each other and eventually began dating. Eventually, I fell in love with her, but our relationship only lasted about a year.

Unfortunately, we broke up on our way to Iowa for a speaking engagement of mine after graduation. What was supposed to be a very fun trip to Iowa turned out in fact to be a horrible one. We stuck it out through the weekend, but I was distracted and my speech was awful. I also slipped and fell on the ice while we were there – an exclamation point to an already bad scene. Perhaps this whole relationship was one of my lessons in life.

On the bright side, if there was one in the whole situation, it helped me grow up emotionally and accept that my being in a wheelchair was an unavoidable issue in our relationship and most likely would be in any relationship I had with any girl. In the first few months of my relationship with her, it didn't seem to be an obstacle, but then I think she realized I needed help with most everything I do and it took a toll on our relationship.

I think that's what eventually broke us up. I think she felt trapped with me. I was like a ball and chain because of the way she'd have to take care of me.

I've had another girlfriend, but it didn't last either. There was a pretty big age difference between us and coupled with my disability, it didn't work out.

I think a lot of girls break up with me or are hesitant to date me because they want to pursue their own dreams. If they get involved with me, they may have to put them on hold or change them, because I need others to do the many things for me which I can't do for myself. If we eventually got married and had children, she'd have to take care of both them and me, so it's a big issue that can't be ignored.

When it comes to women, I need someone who is willing to look past my disability, to see me for who I am - perhaps someone who also has a sense of humor like me. Humor can take the edge off tense situations which can be more frequent when you have a physical disability. In addition to the normal challenges of life, we deal with another level of obstacles to overcome which can be trying on relationships. It will take a special person.

***

My use of humor when interacting with others may be my biggest form of self-expression, but another one of my ways of self-expression is through tattoos. Younger people are into them in a big way these days. They may be like permanent wallpaper, but they are a way to express your deepest feelings in an external way.

I got my first tattoo when I was seventeen. One of my other ones says, "*Life Rolls On*," in cursive, which is a reference to my time in my wheelchair. Another example of my sometimes self-deprecating humor. Another one is, "*What doesn't kill you makes you stronger*." Ha-ha! I had that one done because it was my motto in wrestling. After each match, I got up and just kept on going like the Energizer Bunny. Kelly Clarkson did a good job with the song too!

One of my favorites, though, is a picture of Jesus on the cross. His arm extends down my arm into my hand. It reminds me that Jesus lives in me and I should seek to live in His image. It serves as an everyday reminder to me of that goal.

I also have a lion tattooed on my shoulder because it took a lot of courage, determination, and heart to accomplish what I had. I don't know if I'll get any more ink. These four seem to capture the essence of my life so far.

Brenda:
When it came to Willie dating, each time I would wonder how long each relationship would last before they got tired of his being in a wheelchair. It takes someone pretty special to stay in spite of it. Someone that would say, "I'll stick with you." That wasn't likely to happen in young high school kids who are trying to figure out life in general.

I was so excited about the Iowa trip. We had never done anything like that before where Willie was going to be a featured speaker, so we looked forward to going out there and having a lot of fun. Unfortunately, they broke up on the way out there, so we tried to make the most of it, but Willie was hurt and it showed. His being upset bothered me too, as you would expect it would. When your child is hurting, you're hurting. The trip didn't work out so well. Affairs of the heart are complicated.

When it comes to tattoos, they're mostly a younger generation thing. I generally don't like them, but I've learned now to accept them. It's his thing now. It's just an outward expression. It doesn't really change who he is.

When he got his first one, he waited to call me from the tattoo parlor. He had gone there with a friend of his who was also getting one and his dad. He said, "Mom, I'm here at the tattoo parlor and I'm getting a tattoo. Talk to you later. Goodbye." I thought, *What? Where is this coming from?* Now I love his Jesus tattoo.

15

Willie—In the Aftermath

*You know that the Lord will reward each
one for whatever good they do.*
—*Ephesians 6:8*

Willie:

After my sole wrestling victory, I became more of a recognized person because of my unusual and compelling story and the resulting media exposure. The E:60 ESPN documentary, with its national audience, was by far the biggest catalyst of my being recognized.

Being on a national network, many saw it and asked me to speak to their groups. I was amazed at the response. I didn't know much about public speaking, but I accepted the invitations anyway. I thought I could just tell my story. I feel inspired when I get a request to speak to a basketball or wrestling team, that someone thinks my story is worth repeating and wants to hear it directly from me.

My first trip was a motivational speaking engagement in Iowa, which was at Iowa University, home of the Hawkeyes. It was in November of 2014. This was the trip when I was breaking up with my girlfriend - not good timing. I wish I could have had a do-over on this one. I wasn't very good.

While I was in Iowa though, there were reporters everywhere covering me. That took some getting used to. I didn't want or need that type of attention, it was distracting.

I now know I should spend more time writing down my thoughts before speaking. Too many times I just go off the top of my head. When I wing it like that, it doesn't always go well, while at other times it goes perfectly. It can depend on the audience, but it leaves too much to chance, not to prepare.

The big highlight for me while I was in Iowa is I got to meet the famous wrestler, Dan Gable, in fact, I got to go to his home on Thanksgiving Day. He lives in Waterloo, Iowa, a little town just outside of Iowa City.

I was there because a high school wrestling team in Independence, Iowa had an opening night right before their season just to introduce the team to the fans and each year they invite a guest speaker. Dan had previously spoken to the group, but after they saw my ESPN E:60 video, they invited me to speak.

I was a headline speaker at a banquet. I was amazed when they offered me a $1,500 stipend to speak and put me up in the penthouse suite in a fabulous hotel. Mom and I thought we had died and gone to heaven. We had never stayed in a place like that before.

I don't know how I got invited to Dan's home, but it was very special to meet him, especially since he narrated my ESPN film. Someone was really looking out for me. I was star struck!

When we arrived, Dan walked out and introduced himself to me as if I had no idea who he was – one of the biggest icons of all time in wrestling history. I laughed nervously and replied that of course, I knew who he was.

Dan is a quiet type of man but when he does speak he is funny and easy-going. I couldn't believe where I was. Willie Burton from Kentucky was hobnobbing with Dan Gable. Who would have believed it?

I followed him inside and he took me straight to his awards room, which resembles a museum, and showed me his trophies. The National Wrestling Hall of Fame Dan Gable Museum is in Waterloo, but I'll bet he has more trophies and memorabilia in his home than they have in the museum. I admired each of them and especially enjoyed his stories from his college and Olympic bouts.

He told me one story from when he was wrestling for Team USA in the Olympics. Before the games, the Soviet team vowed to beat him. Not only did they not beat them, but they also didn't even score a point against him in the entire tournament. Now that's a shellacking!

He gave me one of his special autographed wrestling singlets which includes an imprint of his picture. I've been told there were only twenty-seven of them made, and he was gracious enough to present one to me.

His passion for the sport still burns inside him even after all these years. He definitely walks the walk when it comes to wrestling. I was pleased and honored to have met him and it was definitely the high point of my trip.

While we were in Iowa, I also got to meet Benjamin Hupke the famous Iowa high school and college wrestling announcer. He was the 2012 National Wrestling Media Association Broadcaster of the year. It was an honor to meet him and he knew all about me, which was flattering.

Also, while I was in Iowa a reporter for *The Courier*, an Iowa newspaper, asked me how it felt to be the most popular one-win wrestler in history. I told him I didn't know how to answer his question, but it put into perspective for me just how much my one victory meant if I was being mentioned, in his words, as the most popular one-win wrestler in history. The opening line in his article referred to me that way.

I was also invited to Ohio State to speak to their wrestling team. It was an unbelievable experience for me, a high school wrestler, to be speaking to a college team, especially one with the program stature of Ohio State. While I was there, I ran into the Iowa wrestling team, who was there for a Big Ten match. For a guy in a wheelchair, I was really getting around!

I did the speaking circuit because I felt I had an obligation to. I think it's a part of my destiny, to motivate others to overcome obstacles in their own lives. I don't care for public speaking very much though. My speech impediment, the stutter, gets worse when I'm nervous, which can ruin a speech. But as time moved on and I had more public speaking engagements, I got better at it.

***

I'm not sure if my getting out and speaking, or the ESPN documentary alone got me noticed, but somehow I got nominated for some awards I didn't know existed. In February 2016, I was invited to Orlando by the National Consortium for Academics and Sports (NCAS), for their 18th annual Giant Steps Awards Banquet and Hall of Fame Induction Ceremony. It was held at the Orlando World Center Marriott.

This turned out to be my favorite speaking engagement. It was a huge crowd and I got to meet some famous people I could never have dreamed of meeting; even celebrities who had won Super Bowls and had the rings to show for it.

I couldn't believe I was getting an award myself. Getting to mingle with the other award recipients helped boost my self-confidence, to be able to give a good speech.

I was very nervous the entire day leading up to the awards. I could hardly relax. There was going to be over 400 guests in attendance including the celebrities and other notables and there I was, a kid from a high school gym in Fairdale, Kentucky in a wheelchair and with a speech impediment, accepting an award while trying not to make a fool of myself. Oh, the price of notoriety. I just didn't want to mess it up.

Coach Jarvis was with us on the trip, which was a big boost to me. He kept trying to reassure me about my speech, but I was still very nervous.

I also got to meet the parents of Lauren Hill, Lisa, and Brent. Lauren was the young basketball player at Mt. St. Joseph University in Cincinnati, who died from an inoperable brain tumor in 2014 at nineteen years old. They came over to our table and introduced themselves and sat with us before the awards ceremony and I was able to spend some quality time with them.

They told me about how Lauren had won an ESPY award in 2015, which is short for Excellence in Sports Performance Yearly Award, which is presented by the ABC broadcasting network, and previously ESPN, to recognize individual and team athletic achievement during the previous calendar year.

It was very interesting to hear them retell their experience of accepting the award on her behalf. Lisa delivered a tribute to their daughter, in which she asked the audience not to sit on the sidelines, but to get involved to help find a cure for the type of cancer that took Lauren's life.

I never got to meet Lauren, but she must have been an awesome person. Lauren was a tireless spokesperson and advocate for The Cure Starts Now Foundation which is focused on research to find a cure for the DIPG form of cancer that affects mostly younger people. Through her efforts more than $1,700,000 has been raised.

We talked about my disabilities and they were very interested and appreciated my struggles to cope with them. I was impressed with their courage and they told me that hearing and learning about another young person's obstacles helped them cope with their own tragic loss. My goal is to follow their example to inspire, even in some small way, others to persevere over adversity in their lives.

I spoke with Lauren's father, Brent about my speech and how nervous I was with having to speak before such a large crowd. He gave me advice which helped me get through it. He told me the audience isn't there to judge my speaking ability but to hear what I have to say.

His was good advice and helped settle my nerves. I realized that it wasn't important if I made mistakes during my speech, as long as I got my message across in the end. That was his main point and I remind myself of it now each time I have to speak in public.

I was receiving the 2016 *Giant Steps - A Hero Among Us Award*. I was fortunate when it was time for me to deliver my speech. The lights were shining so brightly that I could barely see the audience. It wasn't as intimidating as it would have been had I been able to see everyone staring at me.

Another benefit was that everyone else who received an award was introduced by a person who worked for the organization, but they instead allowed Coach Jarvis to introduce me and stay on stage for the induction. He actually got to hand me my award.

The fact he was allowed to do so, was a surprise to me and I appreciated his being there with me, given our special relationship. For all he went through with me as my coach, it must have been a proud moment for him, too. None of us could have imagined I could have gone from a mat at Fairdale High to a national stage in Orlando. I'm glad we got to share the moment together.

After I was introduced and on stage, the first thing I said was, "Even though I'm the one receiving the award, the real heroes are my mom and dad. If it hadn't been for all they'd done for me in my life, I wouldn't be there receiving the award. They adopted me and raised me despite my serious disabilities. They went above and beyond, so they are the real heroes." It's not so hard to deliver a speech when you can reflect on what they've done for me.

***

In the summer of 2016, I was interviewed online by Scott Casber of Takedown Wrestling a national online radio program dedicated to wrestling. We talked about high school, college, and my ESPN documentary. Scott is a nice, caring man and a great interviewer. He asked me a lot of questions, searching for ways to help me. I appreciate people like him who care about others and use their position and celebrity to help them.

Shortly after the Takedown Wrestling interview, I was interviewed online by Chris Palmore of Gratitude Space. He asked me a number of questions about things I am grateful for and of course I included God, my parents, and Grandpa Puckett first and foremost. Their online article was called *Willie Burton: Wrestling, Heart, Gratitude*, and was well-written. I sometimes wonder how others find me, but I'm grateful that they're searching me out.

Many other articles about me and my journey were written in the aftermath of my victory. Some were on cerebral palsy websites, some on college websites and others on sports websites. Success stories of motivation and determination get a lot of publicity in our otherwise bad news world.

All of these types of interviews, while I can be responding to questions which may inspire others, also inspire me to keep on talking about my life, my struggles, and its rewards.

Brenda:

Willie's popularity and notoriety allowed him to see and experience many places that he wouldn't have been able to otherwise. No one could have predicted this through his wrestling career.

I loved that he was invited on so many trips. I would like to do more traveling with him, but I would need a reliable helper who could help with the lifting. When Joe Jarvis went with us to Orlando, it was great because he helped me with Willie.

In general, it's hard to travel with a disabled person. Special accommodations are always needed. The airlines are fantastic at it, though. They know how to take care of special needs travelers and are very considerate.

The awards he received were fantastic. I was so proud of him. The Giant Steps Award surprised me. I think Willie was awestruck being around all the celebrities because he knew who they were more than me.

He knows about all the athletes and what they've done. He got to see all the rings and trappings of their success. To me, they were just people. I don't mean to take anything away from their accomplishments. I'd constantly be asking him, "Who's that over there?" and he'd tell me who it was and what they had done.

Meeting Lauren Hill's parents was a special moment. Their story is so sad. I can't imagine what they went through losing a child the way they did. I thought they were sweet, special people. They seemed to connect with Willie. It meant a lot to him getting to meet and interact with them.

These recognitions and events have all been good for Willie. It was a great reward for all of his hard work and perseverance. I hope he uses them for motivation for the future to spread the word of his accomplishments for motivation to others.

Epilogue

I lift up my eyes to the mountains—
where does my help come from? My help comes
from the Lord, the Maker of heaven and earth.
—Psalm 121:1-2

My future may be as intriguing to figure out as my past was unusual. Sometimes how we get to a place in our life defines where we go or what we do from there. With my physical limitations, my options are more limited than for others.

After graduation, I tried college at the University of Louisville, but I wasn't ready for college. Throughout all of my educational years, I was looked after by assistants. In college, you're basically on your own. I had trouble adapting. Higher education is getting a second chance in my success as I am attending Campbellsville University, a Kentucky Christian-based college, which has been great for me. I'm praying to be able to focus and complete a degree program in writing and journalism.

As time passes, I keep trying to become more independent both physically and financially. My parents aren't going to be here forever and I have to learn how to support myself. For many with disabilities, once their caretakers pass away or are no longer physically able to provide the necessary care, the person with special needs winds up in a facility for the remainder of their life.

I need to do whatever I can to prevent this from becoming my fate. It may mean trying to improve both my strength and balance, which is getting better each day, for something which may seem as simple as getting on and off the toilet without assistance, still one of my biggest challenges. It has to start somewhere. My basic physical needs are a good place to begin.

***

One of my most important goals in life is to help others overcome their obstacles by providing motivation to them through my struggles. It's easier said than done. You need a pulpit from which to preach to be effective. Mom and I tried to get a ministry going to accomplish this, but it's hard to get any traction when starting one up from scratch. Now I'm looking for a volunteer situation in which to share my life's experiences to help others.

***

Some think part of our journey on earth is not to create our destiny but to discover it. I believe I found mine through my efforts to overcome the obstacles put before me; some I was born with, others were of my own doing. The love of my parents, grandparents, family and friends, the support of my coaches and teammates and health care providers, both my religious and public communities, but above all, the support of my Lord and Savior, Jesus Christ. None of what I have accomplished or will accomplish in my life would be possible without both my earthly and divine support groups. May my heart be filled with the courage of a lion for whatever lies ahead for me as my life's journey continues.

In their hearts, humans plan their course,
but the Lord establishes their steps.
—Proverbs 16:9

Acknowledgments

As much as many of us like to plan our futures, we often find ourselves in places where we never expected we would. Such is the case with me co-writing Willie and Brenda Burton's memoir. I was contacted by Jeff Miller of Cincinnati, Ohio, across the Ohio River from Northern Kentucky where I make my home. Jeff was steered my way by a mutual acquaintance because he was interested in learning how to get a book published.

Jeff had seen the ESPN E:60 segment on TV about a high school wrestler in Louisville, Kentucky who suffered from cerebral palsy. The segment was compelling and drew a comparison between its narrator, Dan Gable, who won every match in college but one, to this kid who lost every match he'd ever been involved in, except one. Jeff wanted to see what he could do to help Willie in any way possible and sought out Fairdale High School's wrestling coaches for information and guidance.

He learned Willie wanted to get his story told to help motivate others to overcome obstacles in their own lives, so he went about looking for information about book publishing. After he contacted me, he sent me the link to the ESPN documentary for some background. I watched it and was immediately overwhelmed by its content and story. I knew I wanted to write Willie's story.

I had written and had published my first novel and was completing the second one at the time so I felt confident in my writing skills, but more importantly, felt I could bring a perspective to the story that maybe another author couldn't. I myself am handicapped because as an infant, I had contracted polio. I felt this gave me an insight into living a life with physical challenges.

I met with Jeff and put on my pitch as to why I was uniquely qualified to work with Willie on his story. We agreed that we should meet with the Burtons and Jeff arranged the meeting and we drove to Louisville one spring Saturday and met for lunch.

Brenda, Willie's mother, Willie, and his coach, Joe Jarvis, met with us and I once again worked to sell myself to the Burtons on my ability to work with Willie on his memoir. Near the end of our conversations Brenda asked in a serious tone, "Okay, I have one question for you. Are you Christians?" referring to both me and Jeff. We both replied we were, to which she replied, "Okay, we want to work with you."

On my drive home to Northern Kentucky, I was both excited about the opportunity and nervous at the same time. The drive gave me time to assess what I had agreed to do and how I would go about accomplishing it.

After I began my work, we realized the story isn't just about Willie and his overcoming the obstacles brought upon him by cerebral palsy, but also of his mother, Brenda, his lifelong supporter, provider and spiritual guide. His story would not be complete without hers.

I owe a debt of gratitude not only to Jeff for steering me to the Burton's but to all of Willie's friends, family, coaches, teammates, his physical therapist and anyone else who devoted their time and energy for my lengthy interviews before I began writing. Their perspective and information on Willie and Brenda were invaluable.

Barry Kienzle